Ionic Cookbook

Over 20 exciting recipes to spice up your application
development with Ionic

Hoc Phan

BIRMINGHAM - MUMBAI

Ionic Cookbook

First published: October 2015

Production reference: 1261015

Published by Packt Publishing Ltd.
Livery Place
35 Livery Street
Birmingham B3 2PB, UK.

ISBN 978-1-78528-797-8

www.packtpub.com

Credits

Author
Hoc Phan

Reviewers
Mike Hartington

Chady Kassouf

Ted Morin

Siva Prakash

Syed Iqrar Raza Zaidi

Acquisition Editors
Aaron Lazar

Rebecca Youé

Content Development Editor
Ritika Singh

Technical Editor
Edwin Moses

Copy Editors
Vedangi Narvekar

Jonathan Todd

Project Coordinator
Judie Jose

Proofreader
Safis Editing

Indexer
Hemangini Bari

Graphics
Abhinash Sahu

Production Coordinator
Komal Ramchandani

Cover Work
Komal Ramchandani

Foreword

This book is the result of 7 months of focused writing and coding by *Hoc Phan*, a talented developer and dedicated writer with whom the Ionic team has collaborated on a past book. Hoc is a dedicated Ionic community member who often speaks about Ionic, and we have the utmost respect for his commitment to teaching others how to use Ionic in really effective ways. This book provides recipes for getting a stew goin' with Ionic!

Hoc teaches developers how to set up a project by installing the Ionic command-line tool (CLI) and creating a new project. He addresses platform-specific styles and how to target each platform with SCSS and JavaScript. He explains how to integrate an Ionic app with Firebase to create a connection to a real-time database. The book covers routing and navigation, as well as running your app on a device (how to target the iOS and Android simulators).

For more advanced developers, the book explains how to integrate device APIs with ngCordova by working with a device's camera. Hoc also addresses the topic of setting up the Whitelist Plugin and working with CSP to make sure your app is secure.

Before I joined Ionic as a core team member and developer advocate, I was a developer and created many internal hybrid apps for my company. Before I began building apps, I evaluated multiple frameworks. Only Ionic provided a complete solution for hybrid mobile development. I could focus on development, and Ionic handled architecture and design.

Ionic offers a complete ecosystem for building performant, beautiful mobile apps using one code base, which saves time and money. We released the stable version of Ionic in May 2015 and have released alpha versions of four of our platform services since then. We plan to continue to support the open source Ionic SDK and release new features, tools, and services. As Ionic's developer advocate, I travel around the US to talk about Ionic and meet Ionic developers, and my favorite part of my job is people's enthusiasm for Ionic. The Ionic community is what makes Ionic great.

You'll find this book to be a great way to get cooking with Ionic and deep dive into the SDK. We're glad to have you as a member of the Ionic community.

Enjoy!

Mike Hartington
Developer Advocate, Ionic.io

About the Author

Hoc Phan is a technologist with a lot of experience in frontend development. He started programming at the age of 12 with Pascal and Assembly on a 486 computer. The way he learned was to start practicing right away even before figuring out concepts. Hoc worked on many JavaScript projects in the past by teaching himself the framework using various online sources. He was one of the first few developers who tested Ionic for its feasibility as a JavaScript replacement of the native language of a device. He wrote the Full Stack Mobile App with Ionic Framework book (for more information, visit `http://www.amazon.com/Full-Stack-Mobile-Ionic-Framework-ebook/dp/B00QF1H380/`), which was very well-received.

He has worked for both start-ups and large companies. By frequently speaking at local meet-ups as well as cloud computing / Big Data industry events and conferences, he learns from other experts. He holds an MBA degree from the University of Washington's Michael G. Foster School of Business.

About the Reviewers

Mike Hartington is a JavaScript developer who has focused on hybrid technologies for most of his career. By working on Ionic, he has been able to take his love of hybrid apps to the next level, focussing on making a power SDK for developers of all skill levels. After working with *Arvind Ravulavaru* on the *Learning Ionic* book by Packt Publishing, he used his knowledge as an Ionic core team member to provide valuable feedback on this book's content. He is thankful to the Ionic community for its support.

Chady Kassouf is an independent iOS and web development expert. He started programming 23 years ago, and he hasn't stopped ever since. Seven years ago, he decided to leave his job as a team leader in one of the leading digital agencies and to start his own business.

His interests apart from computers include arts, music, and fitness. He can be found online at http://chady.net/.

Ted Morin is a software developer with a focus on frontend technologies. He enjoys JavaScript in its many forms and is always exploring new frameworks and tools. He is currently juggling different projects and jobs and pursuing an undergraduate degree in software engineering at the University of Ottawa.

Siva Prakash has been working in the field of software development for the last 7 years. He is currently working for CISCO, Bangalore. He has an extensive experience in the development of desktop, mobile, and web-based applications in ERP, telecom, and the digital media industry. He has a passion for learning new technologies and sharing knowledge thus gained with others. He has worked on Big Data technologies for the digital media industry. He loves trekking, travelling, listening to music, reading books, and blogging.

Syed Iqrar Raza Zaidi is a software engineer with an experience of 4 years. He is currently designated as a Technical Lead at Bond Internet Consultancy LLC in Dubai, UAE. He is an organized, energetic, and dedicated software developer at work who is motivated to be of service by positively contributing towards every piece of work. He has vast knowledge of core JavaScript, and he has dabbled in PHP and Node.js. He built multiple web portals, web applications, mobile hybrid applications, and 2D and 3D games that delight and inform users using the latest web technologies.

He received the Employee Performance Award at Systems Limited in December 2014. He is a Microsoft Community Contributor as well as a technology leader at Mohammad Ali Jinnah University, Karachi, Pakistan.

You can view his LinkedIn profile by visiting `https://pk.linkedin.com/pub/raza-zaidi/6a/201/a62`. If you're interested in his work, you can drop him an email (`razazaidisd@gmail.com`).

Whatever I am today is because of my parents' prayers and my family's love.

---

www.PacktPub.com

Support files, eBooks, discount offers, and more

For support files and downloads related to your book, please visit www.PacktPub.com.

Did you know that Packt offers eBook versions of every book published, with PDF and ePub files available? You can upgrade to the eBook version at www.PacktPub.com and as a print book customer, you are entitled to a discount on the eBook copy. Get in touch with us at service@packtpub.com for more details.

At www.PacktPub.com, you can also read a collection of free technical articles, sign up for a range of free newsletters and receive exclusive discounts and offers on Packt books and eBooks.

https://www2.packtpub.com/books/subscription/packtlib

Do you need instant solutions to your IT questions? PacktLib is Packt's online digital book library. Here, you can search, access, and read Packt's entire library of books.

Why Subscribe?

- ▶ Fully searchable across every book published by Packt
- ▶ Copy and paste, print, and bookmark content
- ▶ On demand and accessible via a web browser

Free Access for Packt account holders

If you have an account with Packt at www.PacktPub.com, you can use this to access PacktLib today and view 9 entirely free books. Simply use your login credentials for immediate access.

Table of Contents

Preface

The world of mobile development is fragmented, with many platforms, frameworks, and technologies. Ionic is intended to fill this gap with its open source HTML5 mobile app framework that lets developers build native-feeling apps using web technologies such as HTML, CSS, and AngularJS. Ionic makes it easy for frontend developers who want to become app developers. The framework provides superior performance with deep Cordova integration and a comprehensive set of tools for prototyping, backend support, and deployment.

This book will take you through the process of developing a cross-platform mobile app using just HTML5 and JavaScript based on Ionic. You will start first by getting familiarized with the CLI and learning how to build and run an app. You will have a look at some common features of real-world mobile apps such as authenticating a user and receiving and saving data using either Firebase or Local Storage.

Next, the book will explain how Ionic integrates with Cordova to support native device features by using ngCordova and takes advantage of the existing modules around its ecosystem. You will also explore the advanced topics related to extending Ionic to create new components. Finally, the book will show you how to customize the Ionic theme and build the app for all platforms.

What this book covers

Chapter 1, *Creating Our First App with Ionic*, introduces the Ionic framework and provides instructions for setting up the development environment and quickly creating and running the first app.

Chapter 2, *Managing States and Navigation*, walks through some examples of how to manage views, states, and the overall navigation within the app. This can be done via either the UI-Router component of AngularJS or the out-of-the-box Ionic directives.

Chapter 3, *Adding Device Features Support*, explains how to use ngCordova to access native device functionalities such as the camera (photo and video), the contact list, e-mail, and map.

Chapter 4, *Offline Data Storage*, explains how to work with persistent data when the device is offline. You will understand the advantages and disadvantages of using Local Storage versus SQLite.

Chapter 5, *Handling Gestures and Events*, explains how a touch event works and how to process these events to create a better interaction or a custom component.

Chapter 6, *App Theme Customization*, provides instructions on how to customize an app for different platforms and create an introduction screen for your own branding.

Chapter 7, *Extending Ionic with Your Own Components*, takes a deep dive into the AngularJS directive and filter customization. You will learn how to leverage events from the core Ionic components and use `requestAnimationFrame` for an improved animation performance.

Chapter 8, *User Registration and Authentication*, explains the different methods that can be used to authenticate a user and how the Firebase authentication system works.

Chapter 9, *Saving and Loading Data Using Firebase*, walks through some examples, such as those related to storing and retrieving data, using Firebase as the backend. Also, you will learn how to manage and render large datasets.

Chapter 10, *Finalizing Your Apps for Different Platforms*, provides instructions for performing the final steps of getting an app published.

What you need for this book

You need the following to work with the examples in this book:

- A Mac computer with Mac OS X Yosemite and root privilege
- Or a PC with Windows 7 or later with Administrator privileges
- iPhone 5 or later
- An Android device with Android 5.x or later (optional)
- A Windows phone device (optional)

Who this book is for

Ionic Cookbook is intended for frontend developers who want to take advantage of their existing skills to develop cross-platform mobile apps. This book will help you become an intermediate or advanced Ionic developer by covering in-depth topics about AngularJS, Cordova, and Sass. Since Ionic is open source, there is a large community that supports this framework for you to continue the learning journey.

Sections

In this book, you will find several headings that appear frequently (Getting ready, How to do it, How it works, There's more, and See also).

To give clear instructions on how to complete a recipe, we use these sections as follows:

Getting ready

This section tells you what to expect in the recipe, and describes how to set up any software or any preliminary settings required for the recipe.

How to do it...

This section contains the steps required to follow the recipe.

How it works...

This section usually consists of a detailed explanation of what happened in the previous section.

There's more...

This section consists of additional information about the recipe in order to make the reader more knowledgeable about the recipe.

See also

This section provides helpful links to other useful information for the recipe.

Conventions

In this book, you will find a number of styles of text that distinguish between different kinds of information. Here are some examples of these styles, and an explanation of their meaning.

Code words in text, database table names, folder names, filenames, file extensions, pathnames, dummy URLs, user input, and Twitter handles are shown as follows: "Ionic Creator allows the user to export everything as a project with all `.html`, `.css`, and `.js` files."

A block of code is set as follows:

```
{
    "name": "myApp",
    "app_id": "",
    "watchPatterns": [
      "www/**/*",
      "!www/css/**/*",
      "your_folder_here/**/*"
    ]
}
```

Any command-line input or output is written as follows:

```
$ ionic start HelloWorld_Blank blank
```

New terms and **important words** are shown in bold. Words that you see on the screen, in menus or dialog boxes for example, appear in the text like this: "Once completed, click on the **Export** button on the top navigation."

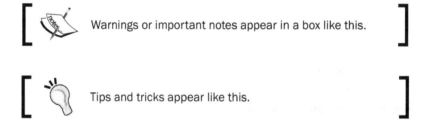

> Warnings or important notes appear in a box like this.

> Tips and tricks appear like this.

Reader feedback

Feedback from our readers is always welcome. Let us know what you think about this book—what you liked or may have disliked. Reader feedback is important for us to develop titles that you really get the most out of.

To send us general feedback, simply send an e-mail to feedback@packtpub.com, and mention the book title via the subject of your message.

If there is a topic that you have expertise in and you are interested in either writing or contributing to a book, see our author guide on www.packtpub.com/authors.

Customer support

Now that you are the proud owner of a Packt book, we have a number of things to help you to get the most from your purchase.

Downloading the example code

You can download the example code files for all Packt books you have purchased from your account at `http://www.packtpub.com`. If you purchased this book elsewhere, you can visit `http://www.packtpub.com/support` and register to have the files e-mailed directly to you.

Errata

Although we have taken every care to ensure the accuracy of our content, mistakes do happen. If you find a mistake in one of our books—maybe a mistake in the text or the code—we would be grateful if you would report this to us. By doing so, you can save other readers from frustration and help us improve subsequent versions of this book. If you find any errata, please report them by visiting `http://www.packtpub.com/submit-errata`, selecting your book, clicking on the **errata submission form** link, and entering the details of your errata. Once your errata are verified, your submission will be accepted and the errata will be uploaded on our website, or added to any list of existing errata, under the Errata section of that title. Any existing errata can be viewed by selecting your title from `http://www.packtpub.com/support`.

Piracy

Piracy of copyright material on the Internet is an ongoing problem across all media. At Packt, we take the protection of our copyright and licenses very seriously. If you come across any illegal copies of our works, in any form, on the Internet, please provide us with the location address or website name immediately so that we can pursue a remedy.

Please contact us at `copyright@packtpub.com` with a link to the suspected pirated material.

We appreciate your help in protecting our authors, and our ability to bring you valuable content.

Questions

You can contact us at `questions@packtpub.com` if you are having a problem with any aspect of the book, and we will do our best to address it.

1

Creating Our First App with Ionic

In this chapter, we will cover:

- ▸ Setting up a development environment
- ▸ Creating a HelloWorld app via CLI
- ▸ Creating a HelloWorld app via Ionic Creator
- ▸ Copying examples from Ionic Codepen Demos
- ▸ Viewing the app using your web browser
- ▸ Viewing the app using iOS Simulator
- ▸ Viewing the app using Xcode for iOS
- ▸ Viewing the app using Genymotion for Android
- ▸ Viewing the app using Ionic View
- ▸ Customizing the app folder structure

Introduction

There are many options for developing mobile applications today. Native applications require a unique implementation for each platform, such as iOS, Android, and Windows Phone. It's required for some use cases such as high-performance CPU and GPU processing with lots of memory consumption. Any application that does not need over-the-top graphics and intensive CPU processing could benefit greatly from a cost-effective, write once, and run everywhere HTML5 mobile implementation.

For those who choose the HTML5 route, there are many great choices in this active market. Some options may be very easy to start but could be very hard to scale or could face performance problems. Commercial options are generally expensive for small developers to discover product and market fit. It's a best practice to think of the users first. There are instances where a simple responsive design website is a better choice; for example, the business has mainly fixed content with minimal updating required or the content is better off on the web for SEO purposes.

Ionic has several advantages over its competitors:

▸ It's written on top of AngularJS

▸ UI performance is strong because of its use of the `requestAnimationFrame()` technique

▸ It offers a beautiful and comprehensive set of default styles, similar to a mobile-focused Twitter Bootstrap

▸ Sass is available for quick, easy, and effective theme customization

In this chapter, you will go through several HelloWorld examples to bootstrap your Ionic app. This process will give you a quick *skeleton* to start building more comprehensive apps. The majority of apps have similar user experience flows such as tabs and a side menu.

Setting up a development environment

Before you create the first app, your environment must have the required components ready. Those components ensure a smooth process of development, build, and test. The default Ionic project folder is based on Cordova's. Therefore you will need the Ionic CLI to automatically add the correct platform (that is, iOS, Android, or Windows Phone) and build the project. This will ensure all Cordova plugins are included properly. The tool has many options to run your app in the browser or simulator with live reload.

Getting ready

You need to install Ionic and its dependencies to get started. Ionic itself is just a collection of CSS styles and AngularJS Directives and Services. It also has a command-line tool to help manage all of the technologies such as Cordova and Bower. The installation process will give you a command line to generate initial code and build the app.

Ionic uses npm as the installer, which is included when installing Node.js. Please install the latest version of Node.js from `http://nodejs.org/download/`.

You will need Cordova, `ios-sim` (iOS Simulator), and Ionic:

```
$ npm install -g cordova ionic ios-sim
```

This single command line will install all three components instead of issuing three command lines separately. The `-g` parameter is to install the package globally (not just in the current directory).

For Linux and Mac, you may need to use the `sudo` command to allow system access:

```
$ sudo npm install -g cordova ionic ios-sim
```

There are a few common options for an integrated development environment:

- Xcode for iOS
- Eclipse or Android Studio for Android
- Microsoft Visual Studio Express or Visual Studio for Windows Phone
- Sublime Text (`http://www.sublimetext.com/`) for web development

All of those have a free license. Sublime Text is free for non-commercial use only but you have to purchase a license if you are a commercial developer. Most frontend developers would prefer to use Sublime Text for coding HTML and JavaScript because it's very lightweight and comes with a well-supported developer community. You could code directly in Xcode, Eclipse, or Visual Studio Express, but those are somewhat *heavy duty* for web apps, especially when you have a lot of windows open and just need something simple to code.

How to do it...

If you decide to use Sublime Text, you will need Package Control (`https://packagecontrol.io/installation`), which is similar to a **Plugin Manager**. Since Ionic uses Sass, it's optional to install the Sass Syntax Highlighting package:

1. Select **Sublime Text | Preferences | Package Control**:

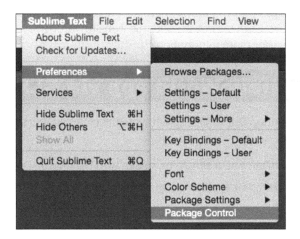

2. Select **Package Control: Install Package**. You could also just type the commands partially (that is, `inst`) and it will automatically select the right option.

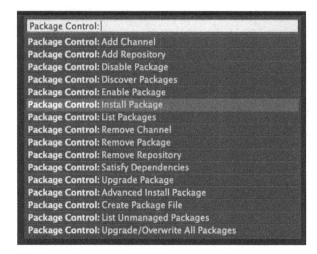

3. Type `Sass` and the search results will show one option for **TextMate & Sublime Text**. Select that item to install.

> Sass
>
> Sass support for TextMate & Sublime Text (2 & 3)
> v2015.01.06.16.00.00; github.com/nathos/sass-textmate-bundle

See also

There are tons of packages that you may want to use, such as Haml, JSHint, JSLint, Tag, ColorPicker, and so on. You can browse around this website: `https://sublime.wbond.net/browse/popular`, for more information.

Creating a HelloWorld app via CLI

It's quickest to start your app using existing templates. Ionic gives you three standard templates out of the box via the command line:

- **Blank**: This template has a simple one page with minimal JavaScript code.
- **Tabs**: This template has multiple pages with routes. A route URL goes to one tab or tabs.
- **Sidemenu**: This is template with the left and/or right menu and with center content area.

There are two other additional templates: maps and salesforce. But these are very specific to apps using Google Maps or for integration with the Salesforce.com API.

How to do it...

To set up the app with a blank template from Ionic, use this command:

```
$ ionic start HelloWorld_Blank blank
```

 If you don't have an account in `http://ionic.io/`, the command line will ask for it. You could either press `y` or `n` to continue. It's not required to have an account at this step.

If you replace `blank` with `tabs`, it will create a tab template:

```
$ ionic start HelloWorld_Tabs tabs
```

Similarly, this command will create an app with a sidemenu:

```
$ ionic start HelloWorld_Sidemenu sidemenu
```

The sidemenu template is the most common template as it provides a very nice routing example with different pages in the `templates` folder under `/www`.

Additional guidance for the Ionic CLI is available on the GitHub page:

```
https://github.com/driftyco/ionic-cli
```

How it works...

This chapter will show you how to quickly start your codebase and visually see the result. More detail about AngularJS and its template structure will be discussed across various chapters in this book. However, the following are the core concepts:

- **Controller**: Manage variables and models in the scope and trigger others, such as services or states.
- **Directive**: Where you manipulate the DOM, since the directive is bound to a DOM object.

- ▸ **Service**: Abstraction to manage models or collections of complex logic beside get/set required.
- ▸ **Filter**: Mainly used to process an expression in the template and return some data (that is, rounding number, add currency) by using the format `{{ expression | filter }}`. For example, `{{amount | currency}}` will return `$100` if the amount variable is `100`.

The project folder structure will look like the following:

You will spend most of your time in the `/www` folder, because that's where your application logic and views will be placed.

By default from the Ionic template, the AngularJS module name is called `starter`. You will see something like this in `app.js`, which is the bootstrap file for the entire app:

```
angular.module('starter', ['ionic', 'ngCordova',
'starter.controllers', 'starter.services', 'starter.directives',
'starter.filters'])
```

This basically declares `starter` to be included in `ng-app="starter"` of `index.html`. We would always have `ionic` and `ngCordova` (as in other examples from this book, although `ngCordova` is not essential). The other modules are required and listed in the array of string [...] as well. They can be defined in separate files.

Note that if you double click on the index.html file to open in the browser, it will show a blank page. This doesn't mean the app isn't working. The reason is that the AngularJS component of Ionic dynamically loads all the .js files and this behavior requires server access via an HTTP protocol (http://). If you open a file locally, the browser automatically treats it as a file protocol (file://) and therefore AngularJS will not have the ability to load additional .js modules to run the app properly. There are several methods of running the app that will be discussed.

Creating a HelloWorld app via Ionic Creator

Another way to start your app codebase is to use Ionic Creator. This is a great interface builder to accelerate your app development with a drag-and-drop style. You can quickly take existing components and position them to visualize how it should look in the app via a web-based interface. Most common components like buttons, images, checkboxes, and so on are available.

Ionic Creator allows the user to export everything as a project with all .html, .css, and .js files. You should be able edit content in the /www folder to build on top of the interface.

Getting ready

Ionic Creator requires registration for a free account at https://creator.ionic.io/ to get started.

How to do it...

Create a new project called myApp:

New Project

Name	
	myApp

Starter Page	✓ Blank
	Login
	Modal
	Side Menu
	Signup
	Tabs

Create Project

You will see this simple screen:

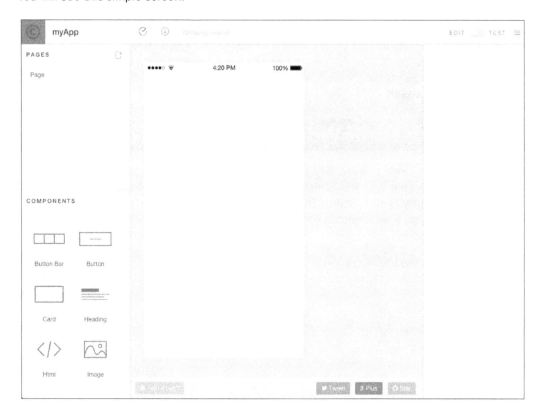

The center area is your app interface. The left side gives you a list of *pages*. Each page is a single route. You also have access to a number of UI components that you would normally have to code by hand in an HTML file. The right panel shows the properties of any selected component.

You're free to do whatever you need to do here by dropping components to the center screen. If you need to create a new page, you have to click the plus sign in the **Pages** panel. Each page is represented as a *link*, which is basically a route in AngularJS UI Router's definition. To navigate to another page (for example, after clicking a button), you can just change the **Link** property and point to that page.

There is an **Edit** button on top where you can toggle back and forth between Edit Mode and Preview Mode. It's very useful to see how your app will look and behave.

Once completed, click on the **Export** button on the top navigation. You have three options:

- ▶ Use the Ionic CLI tool to get the code
- ▶ Download the project as a zip file
- ▶ Review the raw HTML

Export

Ionic CLI   ZIP File   Raw HTML

```
1   <!DOCTYPE html>
2   <html>
3     <head>
4       <meta charset="utf-8">
5       <meta name="viewport" content="initial-scale=1, maximum-scale=1, user-scalable=no,
    width=device-width">
6       <title></title>
7
8       <style>
9         .angular-google-map-container {
10          width: 100%;
11          height: 504px;
12        }
13      </style>
14
15      <link href="/css/preview-frame.css" rel="stylesheet">
16      <link href="/lib/ionic.css" rel="stylesheet">
17
18      <script ionic/angularjs.js
```

Done

The best way to learn Ionic Creator is to play with it. You can add a new page and pick out any existing templates. This example shows a Login page template:

PAGES

▶ Page

▼ Login

▼ form

  ▶ list

  spacer

  button

  button

Here is how it should look out of the box:

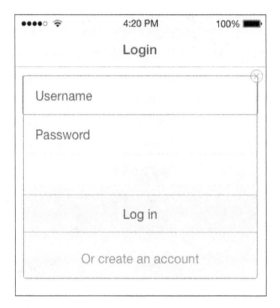

There's more...

To switch to Preview Mode where you can see the UI in a device simulator, click the switch button on the top right to enable **Test**:

In this mode, you should be able to interact with the components in the web browser as if it's actually deployed on the device.

If you break something, it's very simple to start a new project. It's a great tool to use for "prototyping" and to get initial template or project scaffolding. You should continue to code in your regular IDE for the rest of the app. Ionic Creator doesn't do everything for you, yet. For example, if you want to access specific Cordova plugin features, you have to write that code separately.

Also, if you want to tweak the interface outside of what is allowed within Ionic Creator, it will also require specific modifications to the .html and .css files.

Copying examples from Ionic Codepen Demos

Sometimes it's easier to just get snippets of code from the example library. Ionic Codepen Demos (`http://codepen.io/ionic/public-list/`) is a great website to visit. Codepen. io is a playground (or sandbox) to demonstrate and learn web development. There are other alternatives such as **plnkr.com** or **jsfiddle.com**. It's just a developer's personal preference which one to choose.

However, all Ionic's demos are already available on Codepen, where you can experiment and _clone_ to your own account. `http://plnkr.com` has an existing AngularJS boilerplate and could be used to just practice specific AngularJS areas because you can copy the link of sample code and post on Stackoverflow.com if you have questions.

How to do it...

There are several tags of interest to browse through if you want specific UI component examples:

You don't need a Codepen account to view. However, if there is a need to save a custom **pen** and share with others, free registration will be required.

The Ionic Codepen Demos site has more collections of demos comparing to the CLI. Some are based on a nightly build of the platform so they could be unstable to use.

There's more...

You can find the same side menu example on this site:

1. Navigate to `http://codepen.io/ionic/public-list/` from your browser.

2. Select **Tag: menus** and then click on **Side Menu and Navigation: Nightly**.

3. Change the layout to fit a proper mobile screen by clicking on the first icon of the layout icons row on the bottom right of the screen.

Viewing the app using your web browser

In order to "run" the web app, you need to turn your /www folder into a web server. Again there are many methods to do this and people tend to stick with one or two ways to keep things simple. A few other options are unreliable such as Sublime Text's live watch package or static page generator (for example, Jekyll, Middleman App, and so on). They are slow to detect changes and may freeze your IDE so these won't be mentioned here.

Getting ready

The recommended method is to use the `ionic serve` command line. It basically launches an HTTP server so you can open your app in a desktop browser.

How to do it...

1. First you need to be in the project folder. Let's assume it is the Side Menu HelloWorld:

   ```
   $ cd HelloWorld_Sidemenu
   ```

2. From there, just issue the simple command line:

   ```
   $ ionic serve
   ```

That's it! There is no need to go into the /www folder or figure out which port to use. The command line will provide these options while the web server is running:

```
Running dev server: http://localhost:8100
Running live reload server: http://localhost:35729
Watching : [ 'www/**/*', '!www/lib/**/*' ]
Ionic server commands, enter:
  restart or r to restart the client app from the root
  goto or g and a url to have the app navigate to the given url
  consolelogs or c to enable/disable console log output
  serverlogs or s to enable/disable server log output
  quit or q to shutdown the server and exit
```

The most common option to use here is `r` to restart or `q` to quit when you are done.

There is an additional step to view the app with the correct device resolution:

1. Install Google Chrome if it's not already on your computer.

2. Open the link (for example, `http://localhost:8100/#/app/playlists`) from `ionic serve` in Google Chrome.

3. Turn on Developer Tools. For example, in Mac's Google Chrome, select **View** | **Developer** | **Developer Tools**:

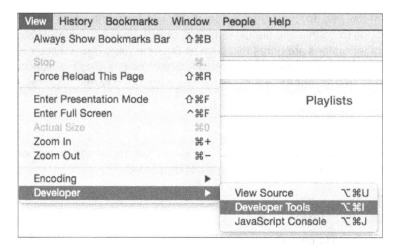

4. Click on the small mobile icon in the Chrome Developer Tools area:

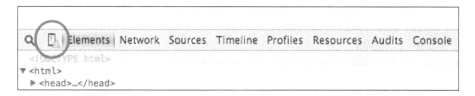

5. There will be a long list of devices to pick from:

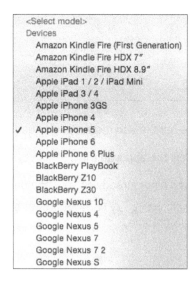

6. After selecting a device, you need to refresh the page to ensure the UI is updated. Chrome should give you the exact view resolution of the device.

Most developers would prefer to use this method to code as you can debug the app using Chrome Developer Tools. It works exactly like any web application. You can create breakpoints or output variables to the console.

How it works...

Note that `ionic serve` is actually watching everything under the /www folder except the JavaScript modules in the /lib folder. This makes sense because there is no need for the system to scan through every single file when the probability for it to change is very small. People don't code directly in the /lib folder but only update when there is a new version of Ionic. However, there is some flexibility to change this.

You can specify a `watchPatterns` property in the `ionic.project` file located in your project root to watch (or not watch) for specific changes:

```
{
    "name": "myApp",
    "app_id": "",
    "watchPatterns": [
        "www/**/*",
        "!www/css/**/*",
        "your_folder_here/**/*"
    ]
}
```

While the web server is running, you can go back to the IDE and continue coding. For example, let's open the `playlists.html` file under `/www/templates` and change the first line to this:

```
<ion-view view-title="Updated Playlists">
```

Go back to the web browser where Ionic opened the new page; the app interface will change the title bar right away without requiring you to refresh the browser. This is a very nice feature when there is a lot of back and between code changes and allows checking on how it works or looks in the app instantly.

Viewing the app using iOS Simulator

So far you have been testing the web-app portion of Ionic. In order to view the app in the simulator, follow the next steps.

How to do it...

1. Add the specific platform using:

    $ ionic platform add ios

 Note that you need to do the "platform add" before building the app.

    $ ionic build ios

2. The last step is to emulate the app:

    $ ionic emulate ios

Viewing the app using Xcode for iOS

Depending on personal preference, you may find it more convenient to just deploy the app using `ionic ios --device` on a regular basis. This command line will push the app to your physical device connected via USB without ever running Xcode. However, you could run the app using Xcode (in Mac), too.

How to do it...

1. Go to the `/platforms/ios` folder.

2. Look for the folder with `.xcodeproj` and open in Xcode.

3. Click on the iOS Device icon and select your choice of iOS Simulator.

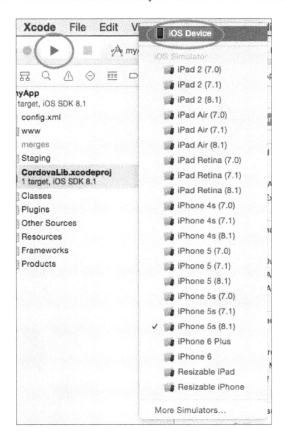

4. Click on the **Run** button and you should be able to see the app running in the simulator.

There's more...

You can connect a physical device via a USB port and it will show up in the iOS Device list for you to pick. Then you can deploy the app directly on your device. Note that iOS Developer Membership is required for this. This method is more complex than just viewing the app via a web browser.

However, it's a must when you want to test your code related to device features such as camera or maps. If you change code in the /www folder and want to run it again in Xcode, you have to do *ionic build ios* first, because the running code is in the Staging folder of your Xcode project:

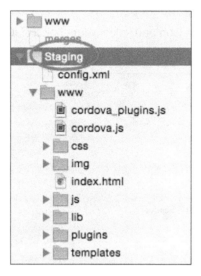

For debugging, the Xcode Console can output JavaScript logs as well. However, you could use the more advanced features of Safari's Web Inspector (which is similar to Google Chrome's Developer Tools) to debug your app. Note that only Safari can debug a web app running on a connected physical iOS device because Chrome does not support this on a Mac.

It's simple to enable this capability:

1. Allow remote debugging for an iOS device by going to **Settings | Safari | Advanced** and enable **Web Inspector**.

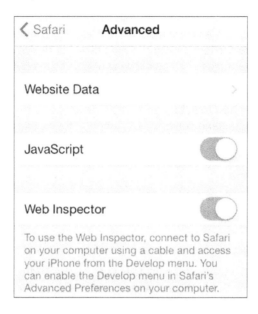

2. Connect the physical iOS device to your Mac via USB and run the app.

3. Open the Safari browser.

4. Select **Develop**, click on your device's name (or iOS Simulator), and click on `index.html`.

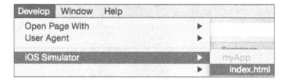

Note: If you don't see the **Develop** menu in Safari, you need to navigate to menu **Preferences | Advanced** and check on **Show Develop** menu in menu bar.

Safari will open a new console just for that specific device just as it's running within the computer's Safari.

Viewing the app using Genymotion for Android

Although it's possible to install the Google Android simulator, many developers have inconsistent experiences on a Mac computer. There are many commercial and free alternatives that offer more convenience and a wide range of device support. Genymotion provides some unique advantages such as allowing users to switch Android model and version, supporting networking from within the app, and allowing SD card simulation.

In this recipe, you will learn how to set up an Android developer environment (on a Mac in this case) first. Then you will install and configure Genymotion for mobile app development.

How to do it...

1. The first step is to set up the Android environment properly for development. Download and install Android Studio from `https://developer.android.com/sdk/index.html`.

2. Run Android Studio.

3. You need to install all required packages such as the Android SDK. Just click on Next twice at the Setup Wizard screen and select the **Finish** button to start packages installation.

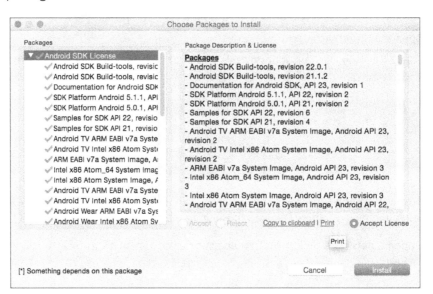

4. After installation is complete, you need to install additional packages and other SDK versions. At the **Quick Start** screen, select **Configure**:

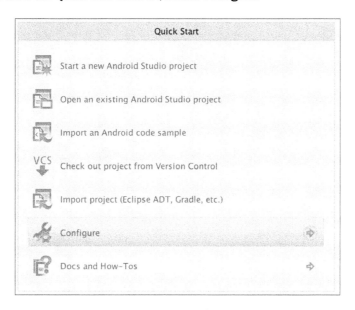

5. Then select **SDK Manager**:

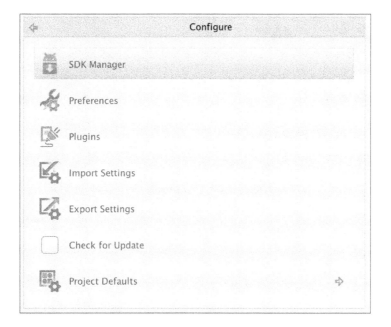

6. It's a good practice to install a previous version such as Android 5.0.1 and 5.1.1. You may also want to install all Tools and Extras for later use.

7. Select the **Install packages...** button.

8. Check the box on **Accept License and click on Install**.

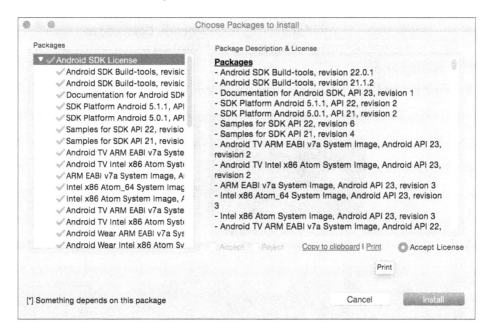

9. The SDK Manager will give you SDK Path on the top. Make a copy of this path because you need to modify the environment path.

10. Go to Terminal and type:

   ```
   $ touch ~/.bash_profile; open ~/.bash_profile
   ```

11. It will open a text editor to edit your bash profile file. Insert the following line where /YOUR_PATH_TO/android-sdk should be the SDK Path that you copied earlier:

   ```
   export ANDROID_HOME=/YOUR_PATH_TO/android-sdk

   export PATH=$ANDROID_HOME/platform-tools:$PATH

   export PATH=$ANDROID_HOME/tools:$PATH
   ```

12. Save and close that text editor.

13. Go back to Terminal and type:

   ```
   $ source ~/.bash_profile
   $ echo $ANDROID_HOME
   ```

14. You should see the output as your SDK Path. This verifies that you have correctly configured the Android developer environment.

15. The second step is to install and configure Genymotion. Download and install Genymotion and Genymotion Shell from Genymotion.com.

16. Run Genymotion.

17. Select the **Add** button to start adding a new Android device.

18. Select a device you want to simulate. In this case, let's select Samsung Galaxy S5:

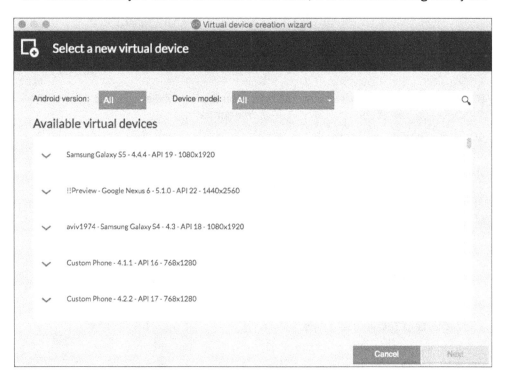

19. You will see the device being added to "Your virtual devices". Click on that device:

20. Then click on **Start**.

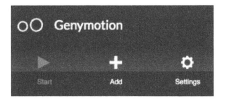

21. The simulator will take a few seconds to start and will show another window. This is just a blank simulator without your app running inside yet.

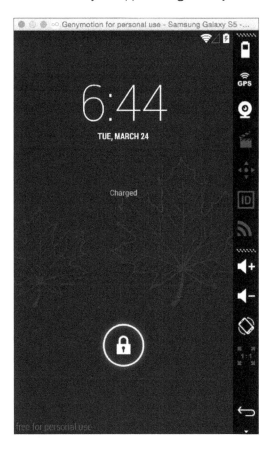

22. Run Genymotion Shell.

23. From Genymotion Shell, you need to get a device list and keep the IP address of the device attached, which is Samsung Galaxy S5. Type `devices list`:

```
Genymotion Shell > devices list
Available devices:

 Id | Select |     Status     |   Type   |    IP Address     |     Name
----+--------+----------------+----------+-------------------+--------------
  0 |   *    |            On | virtual |   192.168.56.101 | Samsung Galaxy S5 -
4.4.4 - API 19 - 1080x1920
```

24. Type `adb connect 192.168.56.101` (or whatever the IP address was you saw earlier from the `devices list` command line).

25. Type `adb devices` to confirm that it is connected.

26. Type `ionic platform add android` to add Android as a platform for your app.

27. Finally, type `ionic run android`.

28. You should be able to see the Genymotion window showing your app.

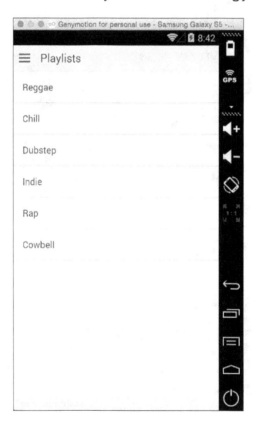

Although there are many steps to get this working, it's a lot less likely that you will have to go through the same process again. Once your environment is set up, all you need to do is to leave Genymotion running while writing code. If there is a need to test the app in different Android devices, it's simple just to add another virtual device in Genymotion and connect to it.

Viewing the app using Ionic View

Ionic View is an app viewer that you can download from the App Store or Google Play. When you are in the development process and the app is not completed, you don't want to submit it to either Apple or Google right away but rather, limit access to your testers. Ionic View can help load your own app inside of Ionic View and make it behave like a real app with some access to native device features. Additionally, Ionic View lets you use your app on an iOS device without any certificate requirement.

Since Ionic View uses the Cordova inAppBrowser plugin to launch your app, all device features have to be "hacked" to make it work. Currently, Ionic View version 1.0.5 only supports SQLite, Battery, Camera, Device Motion, Device Orientation, Dialog/Notification, Geolocation, Globalization, Network Information, and Vibration. It's a good idea to check the updated support list before using Ionic View to ensure your app works properly.

How to do it...

There are two ways to use Ionic View. You can either upload your own app or load someone else's App ID. If you test your own app, follow these steps:

1. Download Ionic View from either App Store or Google Play.

2. Make sure to register an account on ionic.io.

3. Go to your app's project folder.

4. Type `ionic upload`.

5. Enter your credentials.

6. The CLI will upload the entire app and give you the App ID, which is `152909f7` in this case. You may want to keep this App ID to share with other testers later.

```
Uploading app...
Successfully uploaded (152909f7)

Share your beautiful app with someone:

$ ionic share EMAIL
```

7. Open Ionic View and log in if you haven't done so.

8. Select **Load your own apps**.

9. Now you should be able to see the app name in your **My Apps** page. Go ahead and select the app name (**myApp** in this case).

10. Select **Download App** to download the entire app in your Ionic View.

11. After the download process has completed, select **View App** to run the app.

12. You will see the app interface appears with initial instructions on how to exit the app. Since your app will cover the full screen of Ionic View, you need to swipe down by using three fingers to exit back to Ionic View.

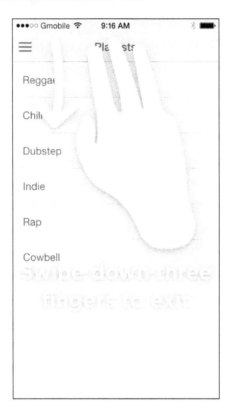

If there is no code update, the process is the same except that you need to select **Sync to latest** at the menu.

In summary, there are several benefits of using Ionic View:

- It's convenient because there is only one command line to push the app.
- Anyone can access your app by entering the App ID.
- There is no need to even have iOS Developer Membership to start developing with Ionic. Apple has its own TestFlight app in which the use case is very similar.
- You can stay agile in the developer process by having testers test the app as you develop it.
- Ionic View has a wide range of device feature support and continues to grow.

Customizing the app folder structure

The structure in starter templates may not be good enough depending on the app. It's important to understand its folder structure to allow further customization. Since the Ionic project is based on Cordova, most of what you see will be either iOS or Android related. This is the breakdown of what is inside the folder:

`platforms/` (specific built code for iOS, Android, or Windows phone)	`lib/`
`plugins/` (Cordova plugins)	`ionic/` (CSS, fonts, JS, and SCSS from Ionic)
`scss/`	`templates/` (UI-router templates)
`ionic.app.scss` (your app's custom Sass file)	`index.html` (main file)
`www/`	`bower.json`
`css/` (your own css)	`gulpfile.js`
`style.css` (processed CSS file that will automatically be generated)	`config.xml`
`img/` (your own images)	`ionic.project`
`js/`	`package.json`

How to do it...

All application logic customization should be done in the `/www` folder as `index.html` is the bootstrap template. If you add in more JavaScript modules, you can put them in the `/www/js/lib` folder.

There is no need to modify the `/platforms` or `/plugins` folders manually unless troubleshooting needs to be done. Otherwise, the `ionic` or `cordova` CLI will automate the content inside those folders.

2
Managing States and Navigation

In this chapter, we will cover the following tasks related to views and states:

- ▶ Creating a tab interface with nested views
- ▶ Creating a multistep form with validation

Introduction

It's possible to write a simple app with a handful of pages. However, when the app grows, managing different views and their custom data at a specific time or triggered event could be very complex. Ionic comes with UI-Router by default. You should leverage this advanced routing management mechanism. In general, the following holds true:

- ▶ A view should have its own state, which is basically a JSON object
- ▶ A route (URL) will point to a view and its assigned controller
- ▶ A state and view should allow nested views so that you can manage hierarchy

Since Ionic introduces many new components, you have to understand how these components impact your app state hierarchy and when each state is triggered.

Creating a tab interface with nested views

This recipe will explain how to work with the Ionic tab interface and expand it for other use cases. For example, it's possible to have additional views (that is, children) within each tab. Since each tab has its own view and state, you can also *watch* the tab change event. The following is the screenshot of the app:

In this app, you will learn the following:

▶ How to create nested views and states

▶ How to create a custom title per view

▶ How to watch for state changes and inject your own conditions depending on the new state

You will also use $ionicLoading, which is a very useful directive if you need to temporarily show some content on the screen (that is, a loading indicator).

Getting ready

Since AngularJS UI-Router comes with the Ionic bundle, there is no need to download an external library. You can test this in a web browser as well.

How to do it...

Here are the steps to create a tab interface with nested views:

1. Create a new app using the *blank* template and go into the folder:

```
$ ionic start Route blank
$ cd Route
```

2. You need to set up the Sass dependencies in the following way because Ionic uses a number of external libraries for this:

```
$ ionic setup sass
```

3. Open the `index.html` file and replace the `<body>` tag with the following:

```
<ion-nav-bar class="bar bar-stable">
  <ion-nav-back-button class="button-icon ion-arrow-left-c">
  </ion-nav-back-button>
</ion-nav-bar>

<ion-nav-view></ion-nav-view>
```

This will set up the view for your navigation, which includes the top bar and content.

4. Open `app.js` and edit it with the following code:

```
var app = angular.module('starter', ['ionic'])

app.config(function($stateProvider, $urlRouterProvider) {
  $stateProvider
  .state('app', {
    url: "/app",
    abstract: true,
    templateUrl: "templates/app.html",
    controller: "AppCtrl"
  })
    .state('app.students', {
      url: "/students",
      views: {
        'students': {
          templateUrl: "templates/students.html",
          controller: 'StudentsCtrl'
        }
      }
    })
```

```
    .state('app.students.details', {
      url: "/details/:id/:age",
      views: {
        'details': {
          templateUrl: "templates/details.html",
          controller: 'StudentDetailsCtrl'
        }
      }
    })
    .state('app.classes', {
      url: "/classes",
      views: {
        'classes': {
          templateUrl: "templates/classes.html",
          controller: 'ClassesCtrl'
        }
      }
    })
    .state('app.classes.details', {
      url: "/details/:id"
    });

  $urlRouterProvider.otherwise("/app/students");
});
```

The `$stateProvider` object is used to set up the routing. You may realize that
there are many template URLs that have not been defined yet. By default, the app
will go to `/app/students`.

5. To define the templates, go back to `index.html` and insert the following code into it:

```html
<script id="templates/app.html" type="text/ng-template">
  <ion-tabs class="tabs-positive">

    <ion-tab title="STUDENTS" ui-sref="app.students">
      <ion-nav-view name="students"></ion-nav-view>
    </ion-tab>

    <ion-tab title="CLASSES" ui-sref="app.classes">
      <ion-nav-view name="classes"></ion-nav-view>
    </ion-tab>

  </ion-tabs>
</script>

<script id="templates/students.html" type=
"text/ng-template">
```

```html
<ion-view view-title="{{ title }}">
  <div class="bar bar-stable bar-subheader">
    <ui-view name="details"/>
  </div>
  <ion-content class="padding content-stable
  has-subheader">
    <div class="card">
      <div class="item item-text-wrap"
      ui-sref="app.students.details({id: 0, age: 19})">
        First Student
      </div>
      <div class="item item-text-wrap"
      ui-sref="app.students.details({id: 1, age: 21})">
        Second Student
      </div>
      <div class="item item-text-wrap"
      ui-sref="app.students.details({id: 2, age: 25})">
        Third Student
      </div>
    </div>
    <button class="button button-block
    button-positive" ui-sref="app.classes">
      View Classes
    </button>
    <div class="hint">
      Click "View Classes" button OR "CLASSES" tab below
    </div>
  </ion-content>
</ion-view>
</script>

<script id="templates/details.html" type=
"text/ng-template">
  <div class="button-bar">
    <a class="button button-calm">ID: {{ id }}</a>
    <a class="button button-calm">Age: {{ age }}</a>
  </div>
</script>

<script id="templates/classes.html" type=
"text/ng-template">
  <ion-view view-title="{{ title }}">
    <ion-content class="padding content-stable">
      <div class="hint">
```

```
        <b>NOTE:</b> No alert showing for
        "app.classes.details" when clicking below
        and no "ui-view" (optional)
      </div>
      <div class="card">
        <div class="item item-text-wrap"
        ui-sref-active-eq="item-active"
        ui-sref="app.classes.details({id:0})">
          Math
        </div>
        <div class="item item-text-wrap"
        ui-sref-active-eq="item-active" ui-sref=
        "app.classes.details({id:1})">
          English
        </div>
        <div class="item item-text-wrap"
        ui-sref-active-eq="item-active"
        ui-sref="app.classes.details({id:2})">
          Science
        </div>
      </div>
      <button class="button button-block
      button-positive" ng-click="gotoStudents()">
        View Students
      </button>
      <div class="hint">
        Click "View Students" button OR "STUDENTS"
        tab below
      </div>
    </ion-content>
  </ion-view>
</script>
```

The templates can be independent files, or they can be included in the `index.html` file itself as a `<script>` tag. You just need to reference it using the `id` attribute.

6. Add the following controller code in `app.js` for the **Students** and **Classes** tab:

```
app.controller('StudentsCtrl', function($scope) {
  $scope.title = '<div class="round-icon"><i class="icon
  ion-person-stalker"></i></div>';
});

app.controller('StudentDetailsCtrl', function($scope,
$stateParams) {
```

```
    $scope.id = $stateParams.id;
    $scope.age = $stateParams.age;
  });


  app.controller('ClassesCtrl', function($scope, $state) {
    $scope.title = '<div class="round-icon"><i class="icon
    ion-university"></i></div>';

    $scope.gotoStudents = function() {
      $state.go('app.students');
    }
  });
```

Note that StudentDetailsCtrl is assigned to templates/details.html in the preceding code. So, it's as simple as passing the scope variables to *render* the data in the view.

7. One more thing that you need to do in app.js is create a high-level AppCtrl object to detect the state change. This is done by using $rootScope.$on for $stateChangeSuccess, as follows:

```
app.controller('AppCtrl', function($scope, $rootScope,
$ionicLoading, $timeout) {

  $rootScope.$on('$stateChangeSuccess', function(event,
  toState, toParams, fromState, fromParams) {

    if (toState.name == 'app.classes.details')
      return;

    $ionicLoading.show({
      template: '<b>Previous state:</b> ' + fromState.name
      + '<br/><b>Current state</b>: ' + toState.name,
      noBackdrop: true
    });

    $timeout(function() {
      $ionicLoading.hide();
    }, 1000);
  });

});
```

8. To make the app look nice, you can customize it by using the following classes in the `ionic.app.scss` file under `/scss`:

```scss
.bar .title {
  overflow: visible!important;
}

.round-icon {
  background-color: $positive;
  border-radius: 50%;
  width: $bar-height;
  height: $bar-height;
  margin-left: auto;
  margin-right: auto;
}

.round-icon > i.icon {
  color: white;
  font-size: 28px;
}

.content-stable{
  background-color: $stable
}

.hint {
  color: #aaa;
  font-size: 14px;
  text-align: center;
}

.item-active {
  background-color: darken($stable, 15%);
}
```

One creative use of classes is shown by the use of the `round-icon` one, as it created a circle around the Ionic icon using `border-radius`.

9. Run the app by using the following command:

```
$ ionic serve
```

If you click on a student's name, it will switch to the `app.students.details` state and pass the parameters (`id` and `age`) to that state. You will also see the loading screen pop up to indicate the previous and current state.

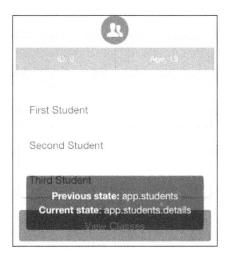

How it works...

At a high level, this is how the app is structured:

▶ The `<ion-nav-view></ion-nav-view>` tag will be replaced by the `app.html` template.

▶ The `app.html` template basically contains just a *skeleton* of `<ion-tabs>`. For each tab, the content will be replaced in `<ion-nav-view name="students"></ion-nav-view>` and `<ion-nav-view name="classes"></ion-nav-view>`.

▶ Each tab has to start with `<ion-view>` as the parent.

▶ For the **Students** tab, there are actually *detail* views nested inside. That's why you use `<ui-view name="details"/>` so that the additional children can replace it.

▶ When you click on a student's name, it actually triggers `ui-sref` directly and passes an expression such as `app.students.details({id: 0, age: 19})`. You basically treat each state name as a function and pass the parameters as a JSON. AngularJS UI-Router will take care of the rest.

▶ You must also tell `ion-tabs` about what to do after each tab in the bottom bar is clicked. That's why you must assign `ui-sref` for the `<ion-tab>` tag as well.

In Ionic, you cannot pass HTML code in the `view-title` directive. The workaround is to fill it with a `scope` variable in the following way so that it can be updated with HTML from the controller:

```
$scope.title = '<div class="round-icon"><i class=
"icon ion-person-stalker"></i></div>';
```

If the user clicks on the button at the bottom to go to another page, it is actually detected automatically by the Ionic tab directive to update the view.

Every time a state is changed, it will trigger a $stateChangeSuccess event after the change is completed. Watching for this event can be tricky because you have to set $rootScope.$on at the *topmost* level (that is, the parent controller). The reason behind this is that this binding must be persistent during navigation. Every time the app state is changed, there is no guarantee that the controller will stay in the memory. It can be destroyed, and it may lose all the binding. The parent controller will always remain persistent during the app's usage.

See also

For further usage of AngularJS UI-Router, you can check out the GitHub repository at https://github.com/angular-ui/ui-router.

Creating a multistep form with validation

Forms are everywhere on the web as well as in mobile apps. If you go through a registration process, it's done using a form. In a shopping cart solution, the user also steps through a multipage form that consists of address, payment information, confirmation page, and so on.

The example in this recipe will explain how to create a form for your app that can be placed in multiple pages and which can have a specific validation for each page. This may sound simple, but it can get complex when there are many pages involved and the user must be available to navigate back and forth. However, you give a lot of flexibility to the users, which results in a better experience.

The app will have four steps. Let's go through the app's functionality:

1. The first step will require three text fields with one field as optional:

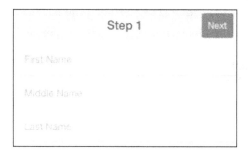

If the user does not fill in the **First Name** and **Last Name** fields, they will see the following error:

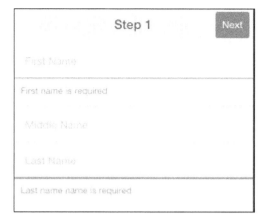

2. Clicking on **Next** will lead to **Step 2**:

There is no required field here, but once the user fills in their email ID, it must be validated:

3. In **Step 3**, the user must check off a checkbox to agree to some terms of service:

Otherwise, it will show an error if the user tries to click on **Done**:

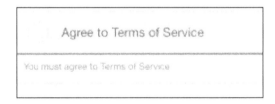

At any step, the user can go back and edit the previous page without an issue. This is usually very difficult if you are not using a Single Page Application framework such as Ionic.

Getting ready

You don't need to test this on a physical device or even a backend server. This example will just simulate the saving of data in the memory and allow you to reset the app at the last step.

How to do it...

Follow these steps:

1. Create a new app using a blank template and go into that folder, as follows:

    ```
    $ ionic start MultistepForm blank
    $ cd MultistepForm
    ```

2. You need to set up the Sass dependencies in the following way:

    ```
    $ ionic setup sass
    ```

3. Open the `index.html` file and replace the `<body>` tag with the following:

```html
<body ng-app="starter" ng-controller="AppCtrl">
  <ion-nav-bar class="bar bar-stable">
    <ion-nav-back-button ng-show="!hideBackButton">
    </ion-nav-back-button>
  </ion-nav-bar>

  <ion-nav-view></ion-nav-view>
 </body>
```

4. Let's ignore the JavaScript part for now and write the templates for the form. Since you need four steps, you have to create each step as a separate page. **Step 1** is structured as follows:

```html
<script id="templates/step1.html" type="text/ng-template">
  <ion-view>
    <ion-nav-buttons side="primary">
      <h1 class="title">Step 1</h1>
      <button class="button button-positive"
      ng-click="submit()" ui-sref="step2">
        Next
      </button>
    </ion-nav-buttons>
    <ion-content>
      <form name="step1Form" ng-controller=
      "Step1FormCtrl" novalidate>
        <div class="list">
          <label class="item item-input">
            <input type="text" placeholder="First Name"
            name="firstname" ng-model="data.firstname"
            required>
          </label>
          <div class="item item-message"
          ng-if="step1Submitted &&
          step1Form.firstname.$error.required">
            First name is required
          </div>
          <label class="item item-input">
            <input type="text" placeholder="Middle Name"
            name="middlename" ng-model="data.middlename">
          </label>
          <label class="item item-input">
            <input type="text" placeholder="Last Name"
            name="lastname" ng-model="data.lastname"
            required>
          </label>
```

```
        <div class="item item-message"
        ng-if="step1Submitted &&
        step1Form.lastname.$error.required">
          Last name is required
        </div>
      </div>
    </form>
  </ion-content>
 </ion-view>
</script>
```

5. The code of **Step 2** is very much similar to that of **Step 1**, but it just has different fields:

```
<script id="templates/step2.html" type="text/ng-template">
  <ion-view>
    <ion-nav-buttons side="primary">
      <h1 class="title">Step 2</h1>
      <button class="button button-positive"
      ng-click="submit()" ui-sref="step3">
        Next
      </button>
    </ion-nav-buttons>
    <ion-content>
      <form name="step2Form" ng-controller=
      "Step2FormCtrl" novalidate>
        <div class="list">
          <label class="item item-input">
            <input type="tel" placeholder="Cell phone"
            name="cell" ng-model="data.cell">
          </label>
          <label class="item item-input">
            <input type="email" placeholder="Email"
            name="email" ng-model="data.email">
          </label>
          <div class="item item-message"
          ng-if="step2Submitted &&
          step2Form.email.$error.email">
            Email address is invalid
          </div>
        </div>
      </form>
    </ion-content>
  </ion-view>
</script>
```

6. **Step 3** has the checkbox that needs to be checked off in order to proceed:

```
<script id="templates/step3.html" type="text/ng-template">
  <ion-view>
    <ion-nav-buttons side="primary">
      <h1 class="title">Step 3</h1>
      <button class="button button-positive"
      ng-click="submit()" ui-sref="done">
        Done
      </button>
    </ion-nav-buttons>
    <ion-content>
      <form name="step3Form" ng-controller="Step3FormCtrl"
      novalidate>
        <div class="list">
          <label class="item item-input">
            <textarea placeholder="Comments"
            name="comments" ng-model="data.comments"
            rows=10></textarea>
          </label>
          <div class="item item-checkbox">
            <label class="checkbox">
              <input type="checkbox" name="tos"
              ng-model="data.tos" ng-click="checkTos()">
            </label>
            Agree to Terms of Service
          </div>
          <div class="item item-message"
          ng-if="step3Submitted &&
          step3Form.tos.$error.agree">
            You must agree to Terms of Service
          </div>
        </div>
      </form>
    </ion-content>
  </ion-view>
</script>
```

7. Finally, **Step 4** is just about the **Done** page, where you render all the data in each page:

```
<script id="templates/done.html" type="text/ng-template">
  <ion-view>
    <ion-nav-buttons side="primary">
      <button class="button button-positive"
      ui-sref="step1" ng-click="reset()">
        Start Over
```

```
      </button>
      <h1 class="title">Thank You</h1>
    </ion-nav-buttons>
    <ion-content>
      <div class="list">
        <div class="item" ng-if="data.firstname">
          <b>First name:</b> {{ data.firstname }}
        </div>
        <div class="item" ng-if="data.middlename">
          <b>Middle name:</b> {{ data.middlename }}
        </div>
        <div class="item" ng-if="data.lastname">
          <b>Last name:</b> {{ data.lastname }}
        </div>
        <div class="item" ng-if="data.cell">
          <b>Cell:</b> {{ data.cell }}
        </div>
        <div class="item" ng-if="data.email">
          <b>Email:</b> {{ data.email }}
        </div>
        <div class="item" ng-if="data.comments">
          <b>Comments:</b> {{ data.comments }}
        </div>
        <div class="item" ng-if="data.tos">
          <b>Terms of Service:</b> {{ data.tos }}
        </div>
      </div>
    </ion-content>
  </ion-view>
</script>
```

8. Edit app.js and create the routes for all the steps, as follows:

```
var app = angular.module('starter', ['ionic'])

app.config(function($stateProvider, $urlRouterProvider,
$ionicConfigProvider) {

  $ionicConfigProvider.backButton.previousTitleText
  (false).text('');
  $ionicConfigProvider.views.swipeBackEnabled(false);
  $ionicConfigProvider.views.maxCache(0);

  $stateProvider
  .state('step1', {
```

```
        url: "/step1",
        data: {
          step: 1
        },
        templateUrl: "templates/step1.html",
        controller: 'Step1Ctrl'
      })
      .state('step2', {
        url: "/step2",
        data: {
          step: 2
        },
        templateUrl: "templates/step2.html",
        controller: 'Step2Ctrl'
      })
      .state('step3', {
        url: "/step3",
        data: {
          step: 3
        },
        templateUrl: "templates/step3.html",
        controller: 'Step3Ctrl'
      })
      .state('done', {
        url: "/done",
        data: {
          step: 4
        },
        templateUrl: "templates/done.html",
        controller: 'DoneCtrl'
      });

    $urlRouterProvider.otherwise("/step1");
  });
```

9. Create `AppCtrl`, which is the topmost parent controller for the app, in the following way:

```
app.controller('AppCtrl', function($scope, $rootScope,
$ionicLoading, $timeout) {
  $scope.hideBackButton = false;
  $scope.data = {
    firstname: '',
    middlename: '',
    lastname: '',
```

```
          cell: '',
          email: '',
          comments: '',
          tos: false
       };

    $rootScope.$on('$stateChangeSuccess', function(event,
    toState, toParams, fromState, fromParams) {
       if ((toState.name == 'done') || (toState.name ==
       'step1'))
          $scope.hideBackButton = true;
       else
          $scope.hideBackButton = false;
    });

  });
```

This controller will handle the form object initialization. Note that the best practice should be to create a separate service/factory to keep the model of the form data. However, to make things simple in this example, you can leverage the AngularJS scope inheritance to share $scope.data in the entire app.

10. Each page will have two controllers: one to manage the entire page, and the other to handle only the form in that page. The reason you have to do this is that <ion-content> creates its own isolated scope. Since your **Next** button is in <ion-nav-buttons>, which is outside <ion-content>, you cannot access child scopes from parent scopes.

```
app.controller('Step1Ctrl', function($scope) {
  $scope.step1Submitted = false;

  $scope.submit = function() {
    $scope.step1Submitted = true;
  }
});

app.controller('Step1FormCtrl', function($scope,
$rootScope, $state) {
  var validate = $rootScope.$on('$stateChangeStart',
  function(event, toState, toParams, fromState,
  fromParams) {
    if (($scope.step1Form.$invalid) &&
    (toState.data.step > fromState.data.step))
      event.preventDefault();
  });

  $scope.$on('$destroy', validate);
});
```

11. A great thing about this method is that your controller tends to look very similar in each page. Here is the controller for **Step 2**:

```
app.controller('Step2Ctrl', function($scope) {
  $scope.step2Submitted = false;

  $scope.submit = function() {
    $scope.step2Submitted = true;
  }
});

app.controller('Step2FormCtrl', function($scope,
$rootScope, $state) {
  var validate = $rootScope.$on('$stateChangeStart',
  function(event, toState, toParams, fromState,
  fromParams) {
    if (($scope.step2Form.$invalid) && (toState.data.step
    > fromState.data.step))
      event.preventDefault();
  });

  $scope.$on('$destroy', validate);
});
```

12. The only difference in **Step 3** is related to how you handle the checkbox:

```
app.controller('Step3Ctrl', function($scope) {
  $scope.step3Submitted = false;

  $scope.submit = function() {
    $scope.step3Submitted = true;
  }
});

app.controller('Step3FormCtrl', function($scope,
$rootScope, $timeout) {
  $timeout(function() {
    $scope.step3Form.tos.$setValidity('agree',
    $scope.data.tos);
  });

  $scope.checkTos = function() {
    $scope.step3Form.tos.$setValidity('agree',
    $scope.data.tos);
  }

  var validate = $rootScope.$on('$stateChangeStart',
  function(event, toState, toParams, fromState,
  fromParams) {
```

```
    if (($scope.step3Form.$invalid) &&
    (toState.data.step > fromState.data.step))
      event.preventDefault();
  });

  $scope.$on('$destroy', validate);
});
```

13. The last **Done** page will basically allow the user to reset the data using `angular.copy` to avoid the *hijacking* of the object reference. Otherwise, you can lose the two-way binding with other pages.

```
app.controller('DoneCtrl', function($scope, $rootScope,
$ionicHistory) {
  $scope.reset = function() {
    angular.copy({
      firstname: '',
      middlename: '',
      lastname: '',
      cell: '',
      email: '',
      comments: '',
      tos: false
    }, $scope.data);
  }

  var validate = $rootScope.$on('$stateChangeSuccess',
  function(event, toState, toParams, fromState,
  fromParams) {
    $ionicHistory.clearHistory();
  });

  $scope.$on('$destroy', validate);

});
```

14. To handle the error message style, edit `ionic.app.scss` and insert the following code in it:

```
.item-message {
  background-color: $base-background-color;
  color: $assertive !important;
  font-size: 12px;
  padding:5px 0px 10px 10px!important;
  border-top: 2px solid $assertive;
  white-space:normal;
}
```

15. From the command line, you can test the app using the following command:

```
$ ionic serve
```

Downloading the example code

You can download the example code files for all Packt books you have purchased from your account at http://www.packtpub.com. If you purchased this book elsewhere, you can visit http://www.packtpub.com/support and register to have the files e-mailed directly to you.

How it works...

To understand how a multistep form works, let's start with the routing system first. When you define a route, you actually assign a piece of data to each route as a step number. This is done using the *data* key, as follows:

```
$stateProvider
.state('step1', {
  url: "/step1",
  data: {
    step: 1
  },
  templateUrl: "templates/step1.html",
  controller: 'Step1Ctrl'
})
```

The reason you need to have this step number is to give the user the flexibility to go back to the previous page without having to complete the form in the current page. You will check whether the user goes back or forward using this step number.

To make a field required, you just need to put the `required` attribute in that `<input>` element, as follows:

```
<input type="text" placeholder="First Name" name="firstname"
ng-model="data.firstname" required>
```

However, in terms of validation, there are two things that you need to do:

```
<div class="item item-message" ng-if="step1Submitted &&
step1Form.firstname.$error.required">
  First name is required
</div>
```

First, you need to make sure that the user actually submitted the form by checking the Boolean value for `step1Submitted`. You may realize that there is no `submit` event here, since the app is just changing the *state* from one page to another. Each state change is basically a `submit` event (except if the user goes back to a previous page). This is why you cannot use the default `submit` event within AngularJS for validation.

The second thing that you should check for validation is any node in the `$error` object of the field. Keep in mind that `step1Form.firstname` here is the `name` attribute of the element, not the `ng-model` directive. Since there may be more validation errors, the only thing that you need to check here is the `required` error.

In the `email` input, the `type` attribute basically dictates its own validation for the email format, as follows:

```
<label class="item item-input">
  <input type="email" placeholder="Email" name="email"
  ng-model="data.email">
</label>
```

In this case, you check for `step2Form.email.$error.email` in the second step.

Handling the checkbox validation can get very tricky. What you can do is detect the click in that box and validate whether it's true or false, as follows:

```
<input type="checkbox" name="tos" ng-model="data.tos"
ng-click="checkTos()">
```

The validation uses the `$setValidity` function from AngularJS to set the value, as follows:

```
$scope.step3Form.tos.$setValidity('agree', $scope.data.tos);
```

So, if this is invalid, the `step3Form.tos.$error.agree` variable will be `true`.

To handle the validation before the state change, you must watch the `$stateChangeStart` event:

```
var validate = $rootScope.$on('$stateChangeStart',
function(event, toState, toParams, fromState, fromParams) {
  if (($scope.step1Form.$invalid) && (toState.data.step >
  fromState.data.step))
    event.preventDefault();
});
```

If the form is invalid, you will trigger `preventDefault()` so that the user will not navigate to the next page.

Also, you should make sure that you destroy the watch at the `$rootScope` level when the controller is destroyed, as follows:

```
$scope.$on('$destroy', validate);
```

If you don't do this, you will end up having multiple *instances* of the function when the controllers are no longer around but the function is tight into `$rootScope` instead. In the `config()` function, this line purposely instructs Ionic not to cache any controller (to avoid issues with old data, binding, and so on):

```
$ionicConfigProvider.views.maxCache(0);
```

The last area to look at is the **Back** button. To avoid showing the **Back** button in the first and last screen (you don't want people to submit the entire form and go back to edit), you need to manually hide it when the correct state matches, as follows:

```
$rootScope.$on('$stateChangeSuccess', function(event, toState,
toParams, fromState, fromParams) {
  if ((toState.name == 'done') || (toState.name == 'step1'))
    $scope.hideBackButton = true;
  else
    $scope.hideBackButton = false;
});
```

Then, from the view, you can use `ng-show` to manage the visibility, as follows:

```
<ion-nav-back-button ng-show="!hideBackButton">
```

See also

It's highly recommended that you explore more on how AngularJS handles validation by visiting `https://docs.angularjs.org/guide/forms`.

3
Adding Device Features Support

In this chapter, we will cover tasks related to leveraging Cordova plug-ins for native device functionalities:

- Taking a photo using the device camera
- Capturing video and allowing playback
- Composing an email with an attachment from an app
- Picking and adding a contact
- Adding Google Maps with geocoding support

Introduction

In this chapter, you will learn how to access some common features of a device such as the camera, contact list, email, and map. Some of those features can be written in a JavaScript-only environment but the performance is not on a par with native support.

Cordova has a very well-supported community with many plugins. You may want to check out `http://plugins.cordova.io/` to understand what is out there. Luckily, you don't need to deal with those plugins directly. You can use the ngCordova (`http://ngcordova.com/docs/`) service on top of Cordova and AngularJS. Keep in mind that even if you use ngCordova, you still need the Cordova plugin because ngCordova just "Angular-izes" the way you interact with it.

Taking a photo using the device camera

For this recipe, you will make an app to take a picture using the device camera or load an existing picture from the device album. The picture could be either in Base64 format or saved in a local filesystem of your app. Here is the high-level process:

- Access the Cordova Camera plugin to trigger camera capture and get the image back in the Base64 or file URI format
- Parse the Base64 data or URI on a `<img>` DOM object
- Display URI if it's in the URI format
- Capture an event of a toggle component
- Display long data (for example, URI) using horizontal scroll

Getting ready

You should have a physical device ready in order to test camera capability. It's possible to just run it via an emulator, but the filesystem support might look different across platforms.

This section also requires Bower to be installed. Bower is a utility to help you manage packages for the frontend. It makes installing packages easier because you don't have to hunt all over the place for correct versioning and dependencies. If you don't have Bower yet, install it using the following command line:

```
$ npm install -g bower
```

How to do it...

Here are the instructions to add camera support:

1. Start a blank project (for example, `Camera`) and go to that folder:

   ```
   $ ionic start Camera blank
   $ cd Camera
   ```

2. Add the Cordova Camera plugin. The default template only has three plugins in the `/plugins` folder: Console, Device, and Ionic.keyboard.

   ```
   $ cordova plugin add cordova-plugin-camera
   ```

3. Install ngCordova:

   ```
   $ bower install ngCordova
   ```

   You should be able to see a new folder, `org.apache.cordova.camera`, being added under the `/plugins` folder.

4. Open `index.html` and add ngCordova in the header:

```
<script src="lib/ngCordova/dist/ng-cordova.js"></script>
```

Note that you have to put `ng-cordova.js` before `cordova.js`. Otherwise, you may have a compile error during the build process.

5. Add a controller in your main parent tag. You can just put it in the `<body>` tag as it's a simple app:

```
<body ng-app="starter" ng-controller="CameraCtrl">
```

6. This is basically the *skeleton* of the app: two buttons in a two-column grid, a list item below with two items (toggle switch and URI display), and `<img>` to show the photo from the device camera. Inside the `<body>` tag, put in the following code:

```
<ion-pane>
  <ion-header-bar class="bar-stable">
    <h1 class="title">Camera</h1>
  </ion-header-bar>
  <ion-content>
    <div class="row">
      <div class="col">
        <button class="button button-calm button-full"
        ng-click="getPicture(1)">Show Camera</button>
      </div>
      <div class="col">
        <button class="button button-calm button-full"
        ng-click="getPicture(0)">Show Album</button>
      </div>
    </div>
    <ul class="list">
      <li>
        <ion-toggle ng-model="item.destinationFILE_URI"
        toggle-class="toggle-calm" ng-click=
        "clickToggle()">Return image file URI</ion-toggle>
      </li>
      <li>
        <div class="item item-icon-left" style=
        "background-color: #f8f8f8;">
          <i class="icon ion-link"></i>
          <ion-scroll direction="x">
            {{ item.imagePath }}
          </ion-scroll>
        </div>
      </li>
    </ul>
```

```
        <img ng-src="{{ item.data }}" width="100%">
    </ion-content>
</ion-pane>
```

Note that the Ionic grid system is very similar to Bootstrap where you have to declare rows and columns. However, Ionic makes it even simpler, so you don't need to specify the column ratio upfront. If you use the `col` class, it will automatically divide the width evenly.

7. Now let's write some code for the `CameraCtrl` controller. Open `app.js` and add your *skeleton* as shown next:

```
var app = angular.module('starter', ['ionic',
'ngCordova']);

app.controller('CameraCtrl', function($scope,
$cordovaCamera) {
});
```

Note that you must include ngCordova as a module dependency in order to use the `$cordovaCamera` service.

8. First, create an object to store the controller data:

```
$scope.item = {
    data: "",
    imagePath: "Photo capture as Base64",
    destinationFILE_URI: false
};
```

 It's a good practice to store data in an object (that is, an item). Image data will be stored in `data`. Every time the user changes the destination type (base64 or file URI) or captures a new image, you need to update `item.imagePath` accordingly. The `destinationFILE_URI` object is just to save the current state of the toggle switch.

9. Now let's deal with the toggle switch by capturing the click or touch event:

```
$scope.clickToggle = function() {
    if ($scope.item.destinationFILE_URI)
        $scope.item.imagePath = "Photo capture as File URI";
    else
        $scope.item.imagePath = "Photo capture as Base64";
}
```

So basically every time the switch state is changed, the controller will update the `$scope.item.imagePath` variable.

10. The `getPicture()` function is the core part of this app because it does a lot of processing:

```
$scope.getPicture = function(sourceType) {
  var options = {
    quality : 50,
    allowEdit : true,
    correctOrientation: false,
    targetWidth: 640,
    targetHeight: 1080,
    destinationType: $scope.item.destinationFILE_URI ?
    Camera.DestinationType.FILE_URI :
    Camera.DestinationType.DATA_URL,
    sourceType : sourceType,
    encodingType: Camera.EncodingType.JPEG,
    saveToPhotoAlbum: false
  };

  $cordovaCamera.getPicture(options).then(function(imageData)
  {
      if ($scope.item.destinationFILE_URI) {
        $scope.item.data = imageData;
        $scope.item.imagePath = imageData;
      } else {
        $scope.item.imagePath = "Photo capture as Base64";
        $scope.item.data = "data:image/jpeg;base64," +
        imageData;
      }
      console.log(imageData);
    }, function(err) {
      alert('Unable to take picture');
    });
}
```

11. When you run the app, you should see the app as shown in the following screenshot:

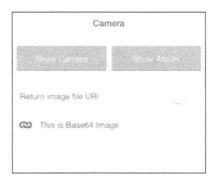

How it works...

Let's start with step 6 of the preceding section.

Although this may look like a lot of *stuffs*, it's actually very simple. Let's start from the top down. The `<ion-header-bar>` tag is just a simple header bar to display the current page. You could even remove it. The `<ion-content>` tag is a wrapper for all app content. So this is the biggest area of your device screen.

```
<ion-pane>
  <ion-header-bar class="bar-stable">
    <h1 class="title">Camera</h1>
  </ion-header-bar>
  <ion-content>
    <div class="row">
      <div class="col">
        <button class="button button-calm button-full"
        ng-click="getPicture(1)">Show Camera</button>
      </div>
      <div class="col">
        <button class="button button-calm button-full"
        ng-click="getPicture(0)">Show Album</button>
      </div>
    </div>
    <ul class="list">
      <li>
        <ion-toggle ng-model="item.destinationFILE_URI"
        toggle-class="toggle-calm" ng-click="clickToggle()">Return
        image file URI</ion-toggle>
      </li>
      <li>
        <div class="item item-icon-left"
        style="background-color: #f8f8f8;">
          <i class="icon ion-link"></i>
          <ion-scroll direction="x">
            {{ item.imagePath }}
          </ion-scroll>
        </div>
      </li>
    </ul>
    <img ng-src="{{ item.data }}" width="100%">
  </ion-content>
</ion-pane>
```

For the image to appear in the `<img>` tag, you need to use `ng-src` instead of `src` alone. The reason is that the `<img>` attribute must be *controlled* by AngularJS in order to have live binding. That's it for the view layer.

The grid system in Ionic is super simple. You can just define it using the `.row` and `.col` classes. The concept is similar to the Bootstrap framework, but you don't have to specify the device size (that is, `-md`, `-lg`, and so on) or even the number of columns. There are two buttons and each is *bound* to the `getPicture()` function. The `<ion-toggle>` tag is simply just an AngularJS directive to create a nicer toggle switch for a mobile device. When the user clicks this toggle button, it will call the `clickToggle()` function.

`$cordovaCamera.getPicture()` is just an abstraction of `navigator.camera.getPicture()` from the Cordova Camera plugin. To post image data to the server, the common scenario is to upload the file from the filesystem. It's not a good idea to send data as Base64 because of the data size, which will increase the original binary size.

You just need to call `$cordovaCamera.getPicture()` with the `options` parameter and callbacks when there is success or an error. Note that it's a better option to reduce the image size and quality, otherwise the app will crash (due to the large memory requirements):

- ▸ `quality` is the quality of the saved image, expressed as a range of 0-100, where 100 is typically full resolution with no loss from file compression.
- ▸ If you want the photo to be automatically saved into the device's album, you can use `saveToPhotoAlbum: true` instead.
- ▸ `destinationType` could be `Camera.DestinationType.DATA_URL` (Base64) or `Camera.DestinationType.FILE_URI` (File URI).
- ▸ The callback will provide the `imageData` variable with the Base64 data or URI. Then you can assign it to the image's `ng-src` attribute.

You could get video in return but it only works if the video is already in the device (when `PictureSourceType` is `PHOTOLIBRARY` or `SAVEDPHOTOALBUM`). This tutorial does not go over the File plugin so that you can access existing photos, as it's a separate topic.

There's more...

It is possible to create Instagram-like filter effects using just JavaScript. You can leverage an existing library such as Filterous (`https://github.com/girliemac/Filterous`) to modify the image canvas directly.

There is an Instagram plugin (`https://github.com/vstirbu/InstagramPlugin`) for Cordova on GitHub. You could write some extra code to pass the image to Instagram. The user must have Instagram installed in the phone first, though. This idea is nice when you plan to do some *cool* image processing (for example, adding funny text) before letting Instagram do the photo filter.

You can even use CSS3 filters (`http://codepen.io/SitePoint/full/KwmeJZ/`) to render in the frontend. However, the disadvantage of this method is that you cannot extract and save the binary of the new filtered image itself.

You could even add Cordova's Social Network plugin and post the resulting images to Twitter or Facebook.

Capturing video and allowing playback

It's possible to capture video using Ionic. There is a different plugin called Cordova Media Capture, which allows more flexible access to audio and video capability. ngCordova also ported this plugin to create the `$cordovaCapture` service (`http://ngcordova.com/docs/plugins/capture/`).

This is very convenient because you just need to call any of those three functions:

- `$cordovaCapture.captureAudio`
- `$cordovaCapture.captureImage`
- `$cordovaCapture.captureVideo`

You could use this plugin for taking a photo as well, but it doesn't have a rich set of features like the Cordova Camera plugin does. The Media Capture plugin only provides access to the video camera to play back or update the resulting video file to a backend server. You cannot use this plugin to perform video processing such as adding text, animation, and special effects.

In this section, you will create a small app with a video capture button. You will learn how to create a video directive so that its playback content can be updated after recording a video.

Getting ready

You need a physical device with functional video capability in order to go through this section.

How to do it...

Here are the instructions:

1. Start a blank project (for example, `Video-Capture`) and go to that folder:

   ```
   $ ionic start Video-Capture blank
   $ cd Video-Capture
   ```

2. Add the Cordova Media Capture plugin:

   ```
   $ cordova plugin add org.apache.cordova.media-capture
   ```

3. Install ngCordova:

    ```
    $ bower install ngCordova
    ```

4. Open `index.html` and add ngCordova in the header above `cordova.js`:

    ```
    <script src="lib/ngCordova/dist/ng-cordova.js"></script>
    ```

5. The body is very simple. You will create a `VideoCtrl` controller that triggers `captureVideo()` when the user clicks on a button. The `<cordova-video>` tag is a new directive to handle video playback.

    ```html
    <body ng-app="starter" ng-controller="VideoCtrl">
      <ion-pane>
        <ion-header-bar class="bar-stable">
          <h1 class="title">Video Capture</h1>
        </ion-header-bar>
        <ion-content>
          <button class="button button-calm button-full"
          ng-click="captureVideo()">Capture Video</button>
          <cordova-video src="data.videoPath"></cordova-video>
        </ion-content>
      </ion-pane>
    </body>
    ```

6. Here is your `VideoCtrl` controller:

    ```javascript
    var app = angular.module('starter', ['ionic',
    'ngCordova']);

    app.controller('VideoCtrl', function($scope,
    $cordovaCapture) {
      $scope.data = {
        videoPath: ""
      };

      $scope.captureVideo = $scope.captureVideo = function() {
        var options = { limit: 3, duration: 15 };

        $cordovaCapture.captureVideo(options).then(
        function(videoData) {
          // Success! Video data is here
          $scope.data.videoPath = "file:/" +
          videoData[0].fullPath;
        }, function(err) {
          // An error occurred. Show a message to the user
          console.log(err);
        });
      }
    });
    ```

Basically you just need to include ngCordova as a module dependency and declare that you plan to use $cordovaCapture in the controller. Then once the button click is triggered, it will call $cordovaCapture.captureVideo() to open up the device video recording. It's possible that the user will record multiple videos, so the returned object (for example, videoData) will always be an array. Your recorded video is stored locally in the app's folder, which you can access via videoData[0].fullPath.

7. For the <cordova-video> directive, you just need to detect when a new video is recorded and add that to the playback:

```
app.directive("cordovaVideo", function () {
  return {
    restrict: 'AEC',
    scope: {src: '='},
link: function(scope, element, attrs) {
      scope.$watch('src', function(newVal, oldVal) {
        if (scope.src != "") {
          // Create a div object
          var div = document.createElement('div');
          div.innerHTML = "<video id=\"myCordovaVideo\"
          controls>"+
                          "<source src=\"" + scope.src +
                          "\" type=\"video/quicktime\">"+
                          "</video>";

          // Delete previous video if exists
          var previousDiv =
          document.getElementById('myCordovaVideo');
          if (previousDiv)
            previousDiv.remove();

          // Append new <video> tag into the DOM
          element.append(div);
        }

      });
    }
  }
});
```

8. For minor styling effects of the video player, you can change `style.css` with the following code:

```
#myCordovaVideo {
  background: red;
  width: 100%;
}
```

How it works...

For step 7, there is a reason you have to write a separate directive to handle the `<video>` tag. AngularJS does not support live binding of the `<video>` tag, so if you write something such as `<video ng-src="yourObject">`, it will not work. You also probably noticed that the directive uses `scope: {src: '='}` as a way to direct the binding to the `data.videoPath` object. This is just a straight assignment by changing the `scope.src` reference to `data.videoPath` so that you can perform `$watch()` on this variable.

The main reason here is that the directive has its isolated scope, which is different from the controller. Another important area here is to call `remove()` on the previous `DIV` element inside this directive. The user may record one video after another. This is simply just a replacement of inner content to show the current video and delete previous ones.

Every time the user records a video, your `$cordovaCapture.captureVideo()` function will return an object in this format:

```
[                                                                                          app.js:9
▼ Object
   end: 0
   fullPath: "/private/var/mobile/Containers/Data/Application/2399FB21-EC24-46E3-B897-F8A889738445/tmp/capture-T0x170078cc0.tmp.pC6clt/capturedvided
   lastModified: null
   lastModifiedDate: 1432526834000
   localURL: "cdvfile://localhost/temporary/capture-T0x170078cc0.tmp.pC6clt/capturedvideo.MOV"
   name: "capturedvideo.MOV"
   size: 268023
   start: 0
   type: "video/quicktime"
 ► __proto__: Object
]
```

You can see that `fullPath` points to a folder with the unique ID of your app. This path is relative to your app. That's why it's necessary to prepend `file:/` in front of the string. Otherwise, the Cordova web app will not know where to find the video file.

Depending on the platform, some parameters such as limit or duration might not be supported by the Media Capture plugin. It's a good idea to visit the GitHub page for the latest information at `https://github.com/apache/cordova-plugin-media-capture`.

There's more...

This section does not cover the process to send or update the video to a backend server because it's not unique to Cordova or Ionic. You just need to use the filesystem path pointing to the video file and upload it as normal.

There are many other free plugin and module alternatives to perform video playback. You could check out Videogular (`http://www.videogular.com/`), which is a very advanced video player written for AngularJS. There is also the Cordova Video Player plugin on GitHub if you want flexibility to access the native player (`https://github.com/macdonst/VideoPlayer`).

Composing an email with an attachment from an app

Your use case may include the ability to let users compose their own email with populated fields. For example, after users perform some specific actions, the app automatically fills in the email receiver, subject, and body to have users send it off. This functionality makes it easy for users so that they don't have to manually compose the email. Many apps use this technique for the *tell a friend* feature.

The code example in this section will use Cordova's Email Composer plugin so that your Ionic app has a standard interface to communicate with the native device feature. You will understand how to attach files such as images to user emails. The image could be a local file in the app filesystem or Base64 string, which is a result from the device camera. The body could even contain HTML tags. Here is the screenshot of the app you are going to build:

However, keep in mind that there is no way to *detect* that the e-mail has been sent successfully. There are many real-world scenarios that you cannot control such as Internet connectivity (that is, Airplane mode), mail server error, and so on. The plugin only provides the callback function when the user closes down their email composer app.

Getting ready

You will need a physical device to test an email. The device must have the email configured in order to send the email.

How to do it...

Here are the steps for composing an email with an attachment from an app:

1. Create a blank Ionic app (for example, `Email`) and change the directory to that folder:

   ```
   $ ionic start Email blank
   ```

2. Install the Email Composer plugin:

   ```
   $ cordova plugin add https://github.com/katzer/cordova-plugin-
   email-composer.git
   ```

3. Install ngCordova:

   ```
   $ bower install ngCordova
   ```

4. Open `index.html` and add ngCordova in the header:

   ```
   <script src="lib/ngCordova/dist/ng-cordova.js"></script>
   ```

5. You will need to add the `EmailCtrl` controller:

   ```
   <body ng-app="starter" ng-controller="EmailCtrl">
   ```

6. Let's show the content of the `email` object in the view. Add the card layout as a way to organize this information:

   ```
   <div class="card">
     <div class="item item-divider">
       {{ email.subject }}
     </div>
     <div class="item item-text-wrap">
       <strong>To:</strong> {{ email.to }}<br>
       <strong>Body:</strong> {{ email.body }}<br>
   ```

```
<img src="img/ionic.png">
<img ng-src="data:image/jpg;base64,{{ Base64Icon }}">
  </div>
</div>
```

The email's to, subject, and body fields are very straightforward. However, this example will show you how to attach a local file (`ionic.png`) as well as a Base64 image. Since the Base64 string is a `Base64Icon` variable, you need to use `ng-src` to properly parse this variable. The `src` attribute can take either URL or Base64 data.

7. Add a button to trigger the email composer, which you will write a function for later:

```
<button class="button button-full button-positive"
ng-click="send()">Send Email</button>
```

8. After the user closes down the composer (regardless of whether the email is sent or not), show a "thank you" note by detecting the `thankYou` Boolean:

```
<p ng-if="thankYou" class="button button-clear
button-positive">
  Thank you!
</p>
```

9. Open `app.js` for editing. Make sure ngCordova is included as a dependency. You can remove the entire `run()` function as there is no need for it.

```
var app = angular.module('starter', ['ionic',
'ngCordova']);
```

10. Create the controller:

```
app.controller('EmailCtrl', function($scope,
$ionicPlatform, $cordovaEmailComposer, Base64Icon) {
});
```

In this controller, you need to do three things:

❑   Check to make sure emails are available on the device

❑   Initialize the email object with some data

❑   Create a `send()` function to trigger the email app

You will create a separate factory called `Base64Icon` later to store the Base64 string.

11. To check for email capability, you need to call the `isAvailable()` function. It's possible that the device is not set up for emails or the email app is not available for some reason.

```
$ionicPlatform.ready(function() {
  $cordovaEmailComposer.isAvailable().then(function() {
    // is available
    console.log('Email is available');
  }, function () {
    // not available
    alert('Email is not available');
  });
});
```

It's important to wrap `isAvailable()` around the `ready()` function. The reason is that when your app starts, it may take a bit of time to load all plugins.

12. Initialize two scope variables: `Base64Icon` and `email`:

```
$scope.Base64Icon = Base64Icon;
$scope.email = {
  to: 'youremail@gmail.com',
  // You can add cc or bcc field with array of emails
  // cc: 'someone@gmail.com',
  // bcc: ['test1@gmail.com', 'test2@gmail.com'],
  attachments: [
   'file://img/ionic.png',
   // file:// is basically your www/ folder
   // You can include any file such as PDF
   // 'file://README.pdf'
   "base64:icon.jpg//" + Base64Icon
   // Note that you must include file name for base64
   such as icon.jpg
   // 'base64:icon.png//iVBORw0KGgoAAAANSUhEUg...',
  ],
  subject: 'Just testing Email Composer Cordova plugin',
  body: 'How are you? Nice greetings from <b>Ionic</b>',
  isHtml: true
};
```

You basically just assign the value of the `Base64Icon` factory into a `scope` variable so you can access it from the view. Attachment is probably the most difficult field to get right. You could attach a local file from the `app` folder. By default, everything is under the `www` folder. So to reference to the `img` folder, you just need to add `file://img/` as the path.

For the Base64 image, you need to have `"base64:icon.jpg//"` as the prefix. The email composer requires a filename in order to attach. If you recall the view, the `src` attribute requires `"data:image/jpg;base64,"` (don't forget the comma at the end) as the prefix instead. So that is the main difference.

13. Create the `send()` function:

```
$scope.send = function() {
  $cordovaEmailComposer.open($scope.email).then(null,
  function () {
    // Callback when user cancelled or sent email
    $scope.thankYou = true;
  });
}
```

This function calls `$cordovaEmailComposer.open()` by passing the email object. Once the composer is closed, it assigns `thankYou = true` in order to show the note in the view.

14. You could include any Base64 string; the example in this book shows the Angular logo. Create `services.js` and make sure to include it in the `index.html` header:

```
app.factory('Base64Icon', function() {
  return "/9j/4AAQSkZJRg…"
});
```

15. You cannot run this app in your browser. So the alternative is to deploy the app via Xcode or TestFlight.

How it works...

The `$cordovaEmailComposer` factory only *translates* three functions from the plugin:

▶ `isAvailable`

▶ `open`

▶ `addAlias`

Keep in mind that although you can include HTML tags in the email body, it does not allow any CSS. Here is the list of tags that you can use:

• `<a href="...">`	• `<h4>`
• `<b>`	• `<h5>`
• `<big>`	• `<h6>`
• `<blockquote>`	• `<i>`
• ` `	• `<img src="...">`
• `<cite>`	• `<p>`
• `<dfn>`	• `<small>`
• `<div align="...">`	• `<strike>`
• `<em>`	• `<strong>`
• `<font size="..." color="..." face="...">`	• `<sub>`
• `<h1>`	• `<sup>`
• `<h2>`	• `<tt>`
• `<h3>`	• `<u>`

See also

▶ You can read the code of this factory directly to understand it, at the following URL:

`https://github.com/driftyco/ng-cordova/blob/master/src/plugins/emailComposer.js`

▶ To see the latest update of `$cordovaEmailComposer`, you can visit the documentation page:

`http://ngcordova.com/docs/plugins/emailComposer/`

▶ There are many other topics that have not been discussed in this section, such as specific problems per platform. The Email Composer's GitHub page is the best place to get the details:

`https://github.com/katzer/cordova-plugin-email-composer`

Picking and adding a contact

Your app sometimes may need to access the device contact list for searching, picking, or adding a contact. This ability can save users time instead of requesting them to enter the information manually.

In this section, you will learn how $cordovaContacts works. Also the app will demonstrate the Ionic tabs feature by creating a navigation view container that has two tabs (a **Find** tab for picking a contact and an **Add** tab for saving a contact). Then UI-Router will *wire* each tab to a specific template. The following is the screenshot of the app:

How to do it...

Here are the steps to follow this recipe:

1. Create a blank Ionic app (for example, Contacts) and change the directory to that folder:

   ```
   $ ionic start Contacts blank
   ```

2. Install the Contacts plugin:

   ```
   $ cordova plugin add org.apache.cordova.contacts
   ```

3. Install ngCordova:

   ```
   $ bower install ngCordova
   ```

4. Open index.html and add ngCordova in the header:

   ```
   <script src="lib/ngCordova/dist/ng-cordova.js"></script>
   ```

5. You will need to add the `ContactCtrl` controller:

```
<body ng-app="starter" ng-controller="ContactCtrl">
```

6. Before writing the controller's code, you need to think how to structure the view. This app will have two tabs. Each tab has its own title bar and content. So let's create the *outer* frame using `<ion-nav-bar>` first:

```
<ion-nav-bar class="bar-positive">
</ion-nav-bar>


<ion-nav-view></ion-nav-view>
```

The `<ion-nav-view>` tag is just a *blank* container like `ng-view`. You will use UI-Router to assign a template into this placeholder.

7. To use Ionic tabs, you need to put the structure in a separate template so that it can be injected into `<ion-nav-view>` at runtime. You could have it in a separate HTML file, but another option is to put the template inside the `<script>` tag:

```
<script id="templates/tabs.html" type="text/ng-template">
  <ion-tabs class="tabs-dark tabs-icon-top">
    <ion-tab title="Find" icon-on="ion-ios-search-strong"
    icon-off="ion-ios-search" ui-sref="tabs.find">
      <ion-nav-view name="find-tab"></ion-nav-view>
    </ion-tab>

    <ion-tab title="Add" icon-on="ion-ios-plus"
    icon-off="ion-ios-plus-outline" ui-sref="tabs.add">
      <ion-nav-view name="add-tab"></ion-nav-view>
    </ion-tab>
  </ion-tabs>
</script>
```

To create tabs, you need to start with the grouping `<ion-tabs>` and then the individual tab item in `<ion-tab>`. The `title` attribute is for the *label* in each tab icon. The `ui-sref` attribute is a part of UI-Router that assigns a state name to that tab. This helps you avoid hardcoding the URL. You also need to give each child, `<ion-nav-view>`, a name such as `find-tab` or `add-tab`. UI-Router will use these names later in `app.js` to properly assign a template to each view.

8. Once you have the *structure*, let's work on the individual content of each tab:

```
<script id="templates/find.html" type="text/ng-template">
  <ion-view title="Find">
    <ion-content class="padding has-header">
      <div class="list card">

        <div class="item item-icon-left">
```

```
        <i class="icon ion-person"></i>
        {{ contactFind.name.givenName }} {{
        contactFind.name.familyName }}
      </div>

      <div class="item item-icon-left">
        <i class="icon ion-ios-telephone"></i>
        {{ contactFind.phoneNumbers[0].value }}
      </div>

      <div class="item item-icon-left">
        <i class="icon ion-at"></i>
        {{ (contactFind.emails[0].value) || "Not
        Available" }}
      </div>

    </div>
    <button class="button button-full button-positive"
    ng-click="pickContact()">Pick Contact</button>
  </ion-content>
</ion-view>
</script>
```

The first tab will allow users to pick a contact and render the information such as name and phone number. Each field can be displayed inside the Ionic's list card. Below the card is just a button to trigger the `pickContact()` function, where the Contacts app will appear for users to pick any contact.

You may notice that each tab's content starts with `<ion-view>` and then `<ion-content>` as a child. The `<ion-view>` wrapper is necessary for Ionic to assign a proper title text on the top bar. `<ion-content>` gives you flexibility to add padding on the top and/or bottom so that there is no content hidden from the header bar.

9. The second tab content will trigger the `addContact()` function to add a contact into the device's contact list.

```
<script id="templates/add.html" type="text/ng-template">
  <ion-view title="Add">
    <ion-content class="padding has-header">
      <div class="list card">

        <div class="item item-icon-left">
          <i class="icon ion-person"></i>
          {{ contactSave.name.givenName }} {{
          contactSave.name.familyName }}
```

```
      </div>

      <div class="item item-icon-left">
        <i class="icon ion-ios-telephone"></i>
        {{ contactSave.phoneNumbers[0].value }}
      </div>

      <div class="item item-icon-left">
        <i class="icon ion-at"></i>
        {{ contactSave.emails[0].value }}
      </div>

    </div>
    <button class="button button-full button-positive"
    ng-click="addContact()">Add Contact</button>
  </ion-content>
 </ion-view>
</script>
```

10. Now you need to edit `app.js` to add the controller. Let's start with the `app` module:

```
var app = angular.module('starter', ['ionic',
'ngCordova']);

app.run(function($ionicPlatform) {
  $ionicPlatform.ready(function() {
    // Hide the accessory bar by default (remove this to
    show the accessory bar above the keyboard
    // for form inputs)
    if(window.cordova && window.cordova.plugins.Keyboard) {
      cordova.plugins.Keyboard.
      hideKeyboardAccessoryBar(true);
    }
    if(window.StatusBar) {
      StatusBar.styleDefault();
    }
  });
});
```

11. Then define the routing config:

```
app.config(function($stateProvider, $urlRouterProvider) {
  $stateProvider
    .state('tabs', {
      url: "/tab",
```

```
        abstract: true,
        templateUrl: "templates/tabs.html"
      })
      .state('tabs.find', {
        url: "/find",
        views: {
          'find-tab': {
            templateUrl: "templates/find.html"
          }
        }
      })
      .state('tabs.add', {
        url: "/add",
        views: {
          'add-tab': {
            templateUrl: "templates/add.html"
          }
        }
      });

    $urlRouterProvider.otherwise("/tab/find");
});
```

The state `tabs` is just a parent state to contain the `tabs` structure. Users cannot just arrive at this state without going to the child state. That's why one of the parameters has `abstract: true` value. Both `tabs.find` and `tabs.add` are children of `tabs`.

When you put a dot notation in the state name, UI-Router automatically interprets it as a child. Note that `find-tab` and `add-tab` are the names you declared in the `tabs.html` template earlier. The `otherwise()` function will tell the app to go to the `find` tab by default:

```
$urlRouterProvider.otherwise("/tab/find");
```

12. Create the controller and include `$cordovaContacts` as a dependency:

```
app.controller('ContactCtrl', function($scope,
$cordovaContacts) {
});
```

13. Within the controller, let's initialize your contact objects:

```
$scope.contactFind = {
  "name": {
    "givenName": "Not",
```

```
      "familyName": "Available"
    },
    "phoneNumbers": [
      {
        "value": "Not Available",
        "type": ""
      }
    ],
    "emails": [
      {
        "value": "Not Available"
      }
    ]
  };

  $scope.contactSave = {
    "name": {
      "givenName": "Student",
      "familyName": "Ionic"
    },
    "phoneNumbers": [
      {
        "value": "(408) 100-2000",
        "type": "mobile"
      }
    ],
    "emails": [
      {
        "value": "youremail@example.com"
      }
    ]
  };
```

The `contactFind` object is used in the `Find` tab, whereas the `contactSave` object is used in the `Add` tab. This is just a basic example to demonstrate the ability to get and add a contact.

14. Write your `pickContact()` function:

```
$scope.pickContact = function() {
  $cordovaContacts.pickContact().then(function(result) {
    // Contact picked success
    console.log(result);
```

```
          $scope.contactFind = result;
     }, function(err) {
          // Contact picked error
          alert('There is an error picking contact.
          Please see console.log');
          console.log(err);
     });
};
```

This function simply triggers `$cordovaContacts.pickContact()` and assigns the result back into your scope object `$scope.contactFind`.

15. To add a contact, call `$cordovaContacts.save()` and pass the contact object:

```
$scope.addContact = function() {
     $cordovaContacts.save($scope.contactSave).
     then(function(result) {
          // Contact saved success
          alert('The contact information has been saved');
          console.log(result);
     }, function(err) {
          // Contact saved error
          alert('There is an error saving contact.
          Please see console.log');
          console.log(err);
     });
};
```

This step requires the user to authorize the app's access to the device's contact list. There is a possibility that the function may fail, so you need to catch that in an error callback. If for some reason you cannot see the new contact Student Ionic being added, it's probably because your device contact hides it. You just need to choose to show all contacts from all groups within the device's contact list app.

16. You cannot run this app in the browser as there won't be a contact list available. It's best if you load the app directly in the device or through TestFlight.

How it works...

There are many fields that can be returned from a contact object. However, they are not supported consistently across all platforms. You may want to check the plugin developer page on GitHub for details at `https://github.com/apache/cordova-plugin-contacts/`.

There is no way to query all contacts and return an array. This is due to privacy. You can only ask the user to pick one contact at a time via the `pickContact()` function.

The user's mobile device may automatically convert a phone number string into a live *click-to-call* link. If this happens, the browser actually modified the DOM and your Angular binding won't work any more as it lost the reference to that new DOM. To prevent26

this scenario from happening, make sure to add the following `meta` tag:

```
<meta name="format-detection" content="telephone=no">
```

You could always manually add the link by using this syntax:

```
<a href="tel:1-408-555-5555">1-408-555-5555</a>
```

It's better to control this process to avoid your DOM being modified by the device.

See also

To stay up to date with the current development of $cordovaContacts, you can visit this:

`http://ngcordova.com/docs/plugins/contacts/`

Adding Google Maps with geocoding support

Many mobile apps today utilize different mapping features such as showing the current location, creating routes, and providing a suggestive business search. This recipe will show you how to use the Cordova Google Maps plugin to provide mapping support. For more information, visit `https://github.com/wf9a5m75/phonegap-googlemaps-plugin`.

You will create an app that can:

- ▶ Display Google Maps in full screen with the ability to detect the current device location
- ▶ Perform geocoding to find the address of any coordinate
- ▶ Add a marker with any text
- ▶ Abstract all mapping functions into a new `<ion-map>` directive and `$ionicMap` delegate

It is possible to use the HTML5 and JavaScript version of geolocation and maps, instead of Cordova plugins. However, you will see a negative impact on performance. It's very obvious that if you use the SDK, map rendering and optimization tends to be faster. In addition, HTML5 geolocation sometimes has some strange bugs that require the user to accept permission twice: once for the app and once for the inside browser object.

Getting ready

The Google Maps plugin requires a Google Maps API key for your project. You need a Google account and login credentials to get started.

1. Navigate to the Google APIs Console at `https://code.google.com/apis/console/`.

2. Create a project if you don't have one yet. Just fill in the fields required:

3. You need to enable the Google Maps SDK for iOS or the Google Maps Android API, or both. It depends on how many platforms you plan to support. Let's select the Google Maps SDK for iOS for this example:

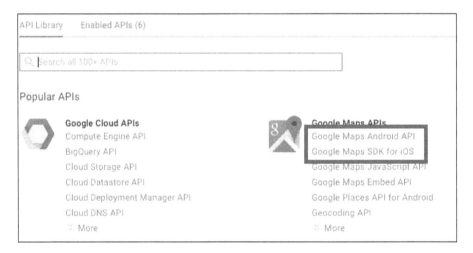

4. Click on the **Enable API** button:

5. Go to **Credentials** to create your own key:

6. Click on the **Create new Key** button under the **Public API Access** section:

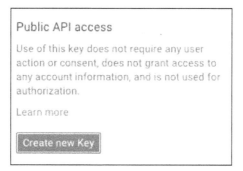

7. Click on the **iOS key** button:

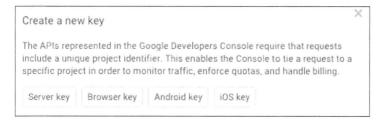

8. Fill in your app's Bundle ID. You might not know exactly what it is yet because Ionic will create a random ID. So just put in `com.ionicframework.starter` and change that later.

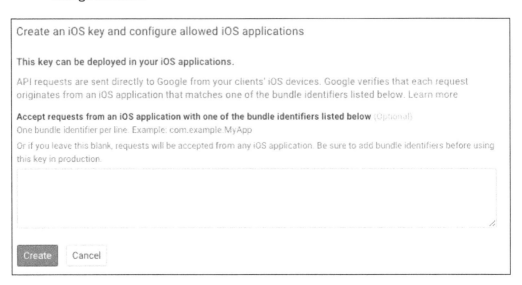

9. Click on the **Create** button.

10. Now you should see the **Key for iOS applications** section like the following:

11. Copy that API key so you can use it to add the Cordova Google Maps plugin.

How to do it...

Let's start an Ionic project from scratch and add Google Maps features:

1. Create a blank Ionic project and go to that folder:

```
$ ionic start GoogleMaps blank
$ cd GoogleMaps
```

2. Install the Google Maps plugin with your copied key replacing `YOUR_IOS_API_KEY_IS_HERE`:

```
$ cordova plugin add plugin.google.maps --variable API_KEY_FOR_
IOS="YOUR_IOS_API_KEY_IS_HERE"`
```

If you do this for both iOS and Android, use the following command line:

```
$ cordova plugin add plugin.google.maps --variable API_KEY_FOR_
ANDROID="key" --variable API_KEY_FOR_IOS="key"
```

3. Since the Google Maps plugin is not part of the ngCordova support, there is no need to install ngCordova in this project. Let's open `index.html` to start working on the view.

4. The first thing you may want to do is to disable telephone number detection in iOS. The reason is that some of the street address matches the phone number format and it may interfere with your model binding. So add the following `meta` tag in your `index.html` header:

```
<meta name="format-detection" content="telephone=no">
```

5. Your UI will consist of a top header bar with one button and the rest of the screen will be Google Maps. You need to assign `GoogleMapsCtrl` first.

```
<body ng-app="starter" ng-controller="GoogleMapsCtrl">
  <ion-pane>
    <ion-header-bar align-title="left" class="bar-stable"
    ng-click="setCenterLocation()">
      <h1 class="title">{{ data.address }}</h1>
      <button class="button icon ion-location button-
      balanced" ng-click="gotoMyLocation()"></button>
    </ion-header-bar>
    <ion-content class="full-height">
      <ion-map width="100%" height="100%" map="map">
      </ion-map>
    </ion-content>
  </ion-pane>
</body>
```

If the user clicks on the header bar, it will get the middle coordinate of the map and return the address at that location. You will write that functionality in `setCenterLocation()` later. The `gotoMyLocation()` function basically gets the current location of the device and shows a marker there with longitude and latitude. The most important component here is `<ion-map>`, for which you will create a directive called `ionMap`. The idea is to call the Google Maps plugin to render the map inside this DOM object.

6. Ionic does not have full screen by default, so you need to customize the style sheet by adding a new class. Let's open `/www/css/style.css` to add a class:

```
.full-height .scroll {
  height: 100%;
}
```

7. Now open `app.js` and start to create a controller, a directive, and a factory:

```
var app = angular.module('starter', ['ionic'])
app.controller('GoogleMapsCtrl', function($scope,
$ionicPlatform, $ionicMap) {
});
app.directive("ionMap", function ($ionicPlatform,
$ionicMap) {
});
app.factory('$ionicMap', function($ionicPlatform) {
});
```

The controller will only have two functions: `gotoMyLocation()` and `setCenterLocation()`, so let's cover that one last. Most of the critical code will be `$ionicMap` as that is your assigned delegate to provide many *map services*.

8. You need to make objects private to keep track of the map object and current center location when the user moves the map around. Put these two lines right under the `$ionicMap` factory:

```
var map = {}
    centerLoc = {};
```

9. This `$ionicMap` factory also returns a list of `public` functions. The skeleton looks like this:

```
return {
  init: function(div) {
  },
  getMap: map,
  gotoMyLocation: function() {
  },
  setCenterLocation: function(callback) {
  }
}
```

You will start writing code for each of the functions.

10. Let's start with the `init()` function, which is when the map is initialized from the plugin.

```
init: function(div) {
  $ionicPlatform.ready(function() {
    // Initialize the map view
    map = plugin.google.maps.Map.getMap(div);

    // Wait until the map is ready status.
    map.addEventListener(plugin.google.maps.
    event.MAP_READY, function() {
      console.log('MAP_READY');
    });

    // When map is moved, get new center location
    map.on(plugin.google.maps.event.CAMERA_CHANGE,
    function(position) {
      centerLoc = position;
    });
  });
  return;
},
```

It's important to call `plugin.google.maps.Map.getMap` on some `div` element because the plugin needs to know where it should render the map. You will call this `init()` function from the directive later. There is even a camera change called `plugin.google.maps.event.CAMERA_CHANGE` so that each time the user moves the map around, you can get the center location and do this assignment: `centerLoc = position`.

11. For the button to trigger the map to move to your location, you can use the `map.getMyLocation()` function of the plugin.

```
gotoMyLocation: function() {

  // Get current coordinate where you are located
  map.getMyLocation(function(location) {
    var msg = ["Current your location:\n",
      "latitude:" + location.latLng.lat,
      "longitude:" + location.latLng.lng].join("\n");

    // Move the camera to your location
```

```
      map.moveCamera({
        'target': location.latLng,
        'zoom': 15
      });

      // Add a marker with position and title text
      map.addMarker({
        'position': location.latLng,
        'title': msg
      }, function(marker) {
        marker.showInfoWindow();
      });
    });
  },
```

The location object returned will contain latitude (`location.latLng.lat`) and longitude (`location.latLng.lng`). To move the camera to anywhere, just call `map.moveCamera` by passing the location coordinate (`location.latLng`). To add a marker, call `map.addMarker` with the position and title as HTML. That's it.

12. The `setCenterLocation()` function performs multiple functions at once. First, it needs to use the `centerLoc` object to add a marker right in the middle of the map. Second, from the coordinate data, Google geocoder will return the official address. Here is the code:

```
setCenterLocation: function(callback) {
  if (centerLoc.hasOwnProperty('target')) {
    var msgCenter = [
      "latitude:" + centerLoc.target.lat,
      "longitude:" + centerLoc.target.lng].join("\n");

    map.addMarker({
      'position': centerLoc.target,
      'title': msgCenter
    }, function(marker) {
      marker.showInfoWindow();
    });

    var request = {
      'position': centerLoc.target
    };

    // Passing longitude and latitude and get back
    the address
```

```
plugin.google.maps.Geocoder.geocode(request,
function(results) {
  if (results.length) {
    var result = results[0];
    var position = result.position;
    var address = [
      result.thoroughfare || "",
      result.locality || "",
      result.adminArea || "",
      result.postalCode || "",
      result.country || ""].join(", ");

      // Trigger callback function to provide the
      address string to the controller
      callback(address);
    } else {
      console.log("Not found");
    }
  });
} else {
  console.log("No location defined");
}
}
```

Note that for `plugin.google.maps.Geocoder.geocode` to work, you must pass the request object with the `position` key. If you send `centerLoc.target` as the parameter, it will not work. Once the address is returned, it will trigger the callback parameter to pass the address string: `callback(address)`.

13. Now that you have the `$ionicMap` delegate defined, this will be your `<ion-map>` directive:

```
app.directive("ionMap", function ($ionicPlatform,
$ionicMap) {
  return {
    restrict: 'AEC',
    link: function(scope, element, attrs) {
      $ionicPlatform.ready(function() {

        // Create a div object
        var div = document.createElement('div');
        div.style.width = attrs.width;
        div.style.height = attrs.height;

        // Add this div to the DOM
```

```
                element.append(div);

                // Turn the div into Google Maps object
                $ionicMap.init(div);
            });


        }
    }
});
```

AngularJS automatically translates the directive naming of `ionMap` into the `<ion-map>` tag in the HTML code. The `attrs` object will contain all the attributes in this tag. So to reference an attribute, you can just call `attrs.width` or `attrs.height`. The goal of this directive is to pass the width and height to this new `div` element and append it in the DOM. Then it would call the `$ionicMap` delegate to initialize the map right on this `div` element.

14. The last part is the easiest component to write. It will be your controller:

```
app.controller('GoogleMapsCtrl', function($scope,
$ionicPlatform, $ionicMap) {
  $scope.data = {
    address: "Tap for address"
  }

  $scope.gotoMyLocation = $ionicMap.gotoMyLocation;
  $scope.setCenterLocation = function() {
    $ionicMap.setCenterLocation(function(address) {
      $scope.data.address = address;

      // Call digest cycle to update $scope.data.address
      $scope.$digest();
    });
  }
});
```

15. If you run the app in your mobile device (not in the browser as the plugin does not work locally), you should be able to see something like the following screenshot:

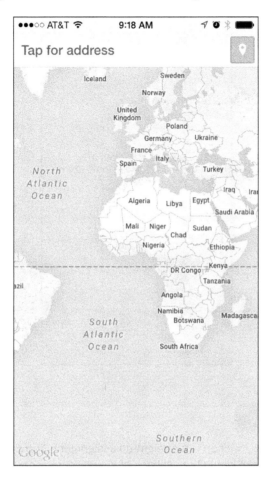

16. Tap the green button for the current location. Tap the top header bar to identify the current address in the middle of the map.

How it works...

The `gotoMyLocation()` function is a straight-up assignment. The `setCenterLocation()` function will get the address within the callback of `$ionicMap.setCenterLocation`. It's important that you trigger AngularJS' digest cycle in the callback because AngularJS will not have knowledge of the variable change when it's outside the controller cycle.

This is to ensure the address change will be updated in the view as well. The `$scope.$digest()` function is just a way to tell AngularJS to re-scan all variables for change detection. If their current values are different from their previous values, then update them in the `$scope` object. By default, Angular triggers the digest cycle in each controller and directive. This *cycle* will do two main things:

▸ Detect changes in scope variables

▸ Update the changes in the UI or other bindings

Although it might seem like there are a lot of moving parts, the basic flow is very simple:

1. Whenever Ionic and Cordova are ready, trigger a callback of `$ionicPlatform.ready` to initialize the map.

2. Create a `div` element and append into the `ion-map` DOM object.

3. Call `getMyLocation` to get location data.

4. If the map is moved, trigger the event `map.on(plugin.google.maps.event.CAMERA_CHANGE,...)` and update the middle coordinate.

5. Call `plugin.google.maps.Geocoder.geocode` to get the address string of the coordinate.

It's important to know that `plugin.google.maps.Map.getMap` does take some time to process, and it will trigger a `ready` event once it has successfully created the map. That's why you need to add an event listener for `plugin.google.maps.event.MAP_READY`. This example does not do anything right after the map is ready, but in the future you could add more processing functions such as to jump to the current location automatically or add more markers on the top of the map.

There's more...

The Cordova Google Maps plugin has many more features such as:

- Show an InfoWindow
- Add a marker with multiple lines
- Modify an icon
- Text styling
- Base64 encoded icon
- Click on a marker
- Click on an InfoWindow
- Create a draggable marker
- Drag events
- Create a flat marker

Since you cannot pop up a `div` element on top of the native Google Maps, the Marker features are very handy. There are some additional scenarios:

- Touch a marker and go to a page: you just need to listen to the `plugin.google.maps.event.MARKER_CLICK` event and do whatever is needed in the callback function.

- Show an avatar / profile image as a marker: `addMarker` does take the base64 image string. So you can pass something like this in the argument `title: canvas.toDataURL()`.

Note that Google has a quota on free API usage. For example, you cannot exceed one request per second per use, and you can only have a couple of thousand requests per day. This quota changes all the time, but it's important to know about it. In any case, if you have problems with your key, you have to go back to the **Credentials** page and regenerate the key. In order to change the key manually in your app, you have to edit `/plugins/ios.json`. Look for two places. The first one is this:

```
"*-Info.plist": {
  "parents": {
    "Google Maps API Key": [
      {
        "xml": "<string>YOUR_IOS_API_KEY_IS_HERE</string>",
        "count": 1
      }
    ]
  }
}
```

And this is the second one:

```
"plugin.google.maps": {
  "API_KEY_FOR_IOS": "YOUR_IOS_API_KEY_IS_HERE",
  "PACKAGE_NAME": "com.ionicframework.starter"
}
```

You just need to edit the `YOUR_IOS_API_KEY_IS_HERE` line and replace it with your new key.

See also

There are lots of ways to work with Google Maps. You can visit the GitHub page of the Google Maps plugin to learn more at `https://github.com/wf9a5m75/phonegap-googlemaps-plugin`.

4
Offline Data Storage

In this chapter, we will cover the following tasks related to persistent data operations:

- Creating a to-do app using ngStorage for Local Storage
- Creating a social networking app using SQLite

Introduction

In this chapter, you will learn how to store and retrieve data from a local device when there is no Internet access. This is important for some apps because of their specific use cases. For example:

- The data does not need to be stored in the server
- It's faster to store data locally and sync it to the server using background processing
- The app must work locally and send data to the server when it's online again

There are several methods for offline data persistence.

- In the past, you probably leveraged cookies in some aspects to store session data such as information regarding whether a user has visited a certain page. Cookies are used for very basic use cases because of their size limitation (4,095 bytes). Cookies are sent to a server on each HTTP request so that the server also has access to this information. This may result in a waste of bandwidth.

- Browsers today have Local Storage support, which is a better method. Local Storage can store up to 5 MB of data and is available only to the client. There are also various libraries supporting Local Storage in the open source community.

- SQLite is also a great alternative for offline data access. However, SQLite is only available as a device-specific feature and not as JavaScript-only. Therefore, in order to use SQLite, you must install a Cordova plugin to support this feature.

In general, you can use the following table to look at criteria, to determine the right technology to use for your offline data storage:

Criteria	Cookie	Local Storage	SQLite
Data available on the server side	Yes	No	No
Data size	<4 KB	<5 MB	This depends on the device space (can be in terabytes)
JavaScript-only	Yes	Yes	The Cordova plugin is required
Older device support	Yes	Yes	You may see performance issues
Complex many-to-many relationships	No	You may see performance issues	Yes

This chapter will go into detail regarding how to work with both Local Storage and SQLite.

Creating a to-do app using ngStorage for Local Storage

There are many to-do apps out there, but it could get very complex when you just want to explore one capability of the platform or framework. The example in this recipe will leverage the idea of a to-do app to explain how Local Storage works. Most apps use Local Storage as a method to ensure that the app data is persistent and available offline. You will learn some basic knowledge about how to manipulate data by adding, editing, and deleting them. These are some very common operations for any app.

Here is the high-level process:

- ▶ Initialize a Local Storage object with some sample data
- ▶ Render an array of objects in the frontend
- ▶ Allow the user to delete an item in the array and then update Local Storage
- ▶ Allow the user to edit an item in the array by using $ionicPopup
- ▶ Allow the user to move the position of an item by manipulating the Local Storage array

You will not access the localStorage object directly. Instead, you will use an existing module called ngStorage. This module is compatible with AngularJS and works very well in an Ionic app.

The following is a screenshot of the to-do app that you are going to build:

Getting ready

You don't need to test Local Storage on a physical device, because it will work in a browser. If you want to test the offline capability, you can even turn off the network connectivity and the app should still be functional.

How to do it...

Follow these steps to create a to-do app:

1. Start a blank project (for example, `LocalStorage`) and go to that folder, as follows:

    ```
    $ ionic start LocalStorage blank
    $ cd LocalStorage
    ```

2. Install ngStorage:

    ```
    $ bower install ngstorage
    ```

3. Add ngStorage in the header above `app.js`:

    ```
    <script src="lib/ngstorage/ngStorage.js"></script>
    ```

4. Add a controller in the `<body>` tag or a parent tag:

```
<body ng-app="starter" ng-controller="MainCtrl">
```

The body will consist of the header bar and content area. The header bar will show the **Delete** and **Reorder** button. The content area will show your to-do list.

5. Create a header bar within the `<body>` tag:

```
<ion-header-bar class="bar-positive">
  <div class="buttons">
    <button class="button button-icon icon
    ion-ios-minus-outline"
      ng-click="data.showDelete = !data.showDelete;
      data.showReorder = false"></button>
  </div>
  <h1 class="title">Todo List</h1>
  <div class="buttons">
    <button class="button" ng-click="data.showDelete =
    false; data.showReorder = !data.showReorder">
      Reorder
    </button>
  </div>
</ion-header-bar>
```

This header bar is very simple. Both the **Delete** and **Reorder** buttons are *wired* with some variables. Delete and reorder are two different *modes* that the user can do only once at a time. The two Boolean variables, `data.showDelete` and `data.showReorder`, will be passed on to the `<ion-list>` directive later as a *toggle* for the action.

6. Now, let's add the `<ion-content>` tag to display the to-do list:

```
<ion-content>
  <ion-list show-delete="data.showDelete"
  show-reorder="data.showReorder">

    <ion-item ng-repeat="item in $storage.items"
    item="item" class="item-remove-animate">
      {{ item.label }}
      <ion-delete-button class="ion-minus-circled"
      ng-click="onItemDelete(item)">
      </ion-delete-button>
      <ion-option-button class="button-assertive"
      ng-click="edit($index)">
        Edit
      </ion-option-button>
```

```
  <ion-reorder-button class="ion-navicon"
  on-reorder="moveItem(item, $fromIndex,
  $toIndex)"></ion-reorder-button>
</ion-item>
<div class="item item-input-inset">
  <label class="item-input-wrapper">
    <input type="text" placeholder="Todo item"
    ng-model="data.item">
  </label>
  <button class="button button-small"
  ng-click="addItem()">
    Add
  </button>
</div>

</ion-list>
</ion-content>
```

The last row will allow the user to add a new to-do item. This is wrapped within the `<div class="item item-input-inset">` element. Each `<ion-item>` element is just a `div` element with classes. In this case, you shouldn't use the `<ion-item>` directive itself, because you need to customize the internal components. This last item will contain only an input box and a button.

7. The next step is to create a controller to handle all the events. Open app.js to modify its content by first adding ngStorage as the dependency:

```
var app = angular.module('starter', ['ionic',
'ngStorage']);
```

8. The `MainCtrl` controller will need to have three dependencies: `$ionicPopup` to handle the edit popup, `$ionicListDelegate` to let you trigger the close of the **Option** button, and `$localStorage` from ngStorage:

```
app.controller('MainCtrl', function($scope, $ionicPopup,
$ionicListDelegate, $localStorage) {
});
```

9. First, you need to initialize this controller, as follows:

```
$scope.$storage = $localStorage.$default({
  items: [
    { label: 'First todo item' },
    { label: 'Second todo item' },
    { label: 'Third todo item' },
```

```
    { label: 'Fourth todo item' },
    { label: 'Fifth todo item' }
  ]
});
```

 There is no need to initialize `showDelete` or `showReorder` because by default, we want them to be false anyway. In JavaScript, an undefined variable is false.

To use Local Storage, you just need to assign a scope variable to `$localStorage`. ngStorage will take care of the binding and updating of the `$scope` object. There is no need to call `getter()` or `setter()` as you may have seen in some other solutions. To assign a default value, you just need to call `$default()`. You can treat Local Storage like a NoSQL solution, as you can just store any object with any structure.

10. To edit an item, the controller will call `$ionicPopup` to show a popup with one field to edit:

```
$scope.edit = function(index) {
  $scope.editItem = {label:
  $scope.$storage.items[index].label};
  var itemPopup = $ionicPopup.show({
    template: '<input type="text"
  ng-model="editItem.label">',
    title: 'Edit Todo',
    scope: $scope,
    buttons: [
      { text: 'Cancel' },
      {
        text: '<b>Save</b>',
        type: 'button-positive',
        onTap: function(e) {
          if (!$scope.editItem.label) {
            e.preventDefault();
          } else {
            $scope.$storage.items[index].label =
            $scope.editItem.label;
```

```
        return $scope.editItem;
      }
    }
  }
]
});
itemPopup.then(function(res) {
  $ionicListDelegate.closeOptionButtons();
});
};
```

In the view, when the **Edit** button is clicked, you also pass the index of the current item in the `ng-click="edit($index)"` array. By doing so, you can access the *label* of that object by calling `$scope.$storage.items[index].label`. That way, when the popup appears, it will show the value of the current item, which will allow the user to edit the item.

11. To move or reorder an item, the `moveItem()` function will manipulate the array:

```
$scope.moveItem = function(item, fromIndex, toIndex) {
  $scope.$storage.items.splice(fromIndex, 1);
  $scope.$storage.items.splice(toIndex, 0, item);
};
```

The reordering action is done by using an array's `splice()` function, which is basically a simple *trick* that can be used to delete an array item and insert it back in a different index.

12. Next, to delete an item, the `onItemDelete()` function will handle `splice()` of the exact item index:

```
$scope.onItemDelete = function(item) {
  $scope.$storage.items.splice($scope.$storage.
  items.indexOf(item), 1);
};
```

13. Finally, to add an item, you can just push the object into the `$storage.items` array:

```
$scope.addItem = function() {
  $scope.$storage.items.push({label: $scope.data.item});
  $scope.data.item = '';
}
```

After it's pushed, just reset `$scope.data.item` to an empty string again.

14. That's it. If you test the app in the browser via `ionic serve`, you should be able to see the Local Storage object being stored. Navigate to the **Resources** tab, expand **Local Storage**, and click on `http://localhost:8100/`, as follows:

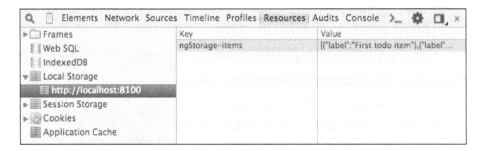

How it works...

This recipe introduced the usage of `<ion-list>`. This directive has two attributes: `show-delete` and `show-reorder` in the view. If the value is `true`, it will enable that feature. If you pass a variable to these attributes, they can be turned on and off programmatically. Under `<ion-list>`, there are two components: a list of the existing to-do items from Local Storage and an input box that can be used to add a new to-do item.

You can loop through a Local Storage object (`$storage.items`) just like any `$scope` object. The `$storage` object defined in the controller is basically a Local Storage object created by ngStorage, which makes it a lot easier to manipulate variables in an AngularJS way. To ensure that there are some elements that can be used to handle delete and reorder, you need to put the `<ion-delete-button>` and `<ion-reorder-button>` directives within `<ion-item>`. This includes an individual button for each item. Besides these *special function* buttons, you can add custom buttons using `<ion-option-button>`. All of these buttons must of course be assigned with `ng-click` to process the event.

In this recipe, `$ionicPopup` was also introduced. This is an out-of-the-box Ionic delegate, where you can control a custom pop-up dialog. When you click on the popup's button, `onTap` will be triggered. You don't want the user to close and save the to-do item as an empty string. That's why you need to call `e.preventDefault()` in order to ignore the tap event. Otherwise, you need to reassign the new label to `$scope.$storage.items[index].label`. In addition to this, the reason behind why you need to call `itemPopup.then()` is that when you click on the option of the `<ion-item>`, it doesn't close automatically. Therefore, you need to close this button once the user returns from the popup.

Looking under the hood, ngStorage just leverages the native `window.localStorage` object. There is no cookie failover, because most browsers already have support for the Local Storage technology. ngStorage abstracts all the steps to convert JSON to a string and vice versa. It also sets up `$watch` for the `$scope` object to detect changes in the Local Storage objects. That's why you can use `$scope.$storage` in the same way as the normal AngularJS `$scope` variables.

There's more...

For iOS devices, the data in Local Storage will be backed up to iCloud automatically by default. This means that the app data will be persistent even if the user updates the app or restores the entire iPhone. To disable automatic backup, you need to modify the `config.xml` of your Ionic project, as follows:

```
<preference name="BackupWebStorage" value="none" />
```

If you want to completely erase all the Local Storage data of your app, use the `$reset()` function, as follows:

```
$localStorage.$reset();
```

See also

For more information about ngStorage, you can access their GitHub project at `https://github.com/gsklee/ngStorage`.

Creating a social networking app using SQLite

This recipe will discuss how you can build a complex relational database app using SQLite. In a real-world scenario, the database usually stays in the backend, where it's more feasible to process a large amount of data for multiple users.

However, there are some cases where the app just needs to work on a limited set of data in the local client device. While it's possible to leverage Local Storage, you will run into the 5 MB limitation of Local Storage very quickly. In addition, you can take advantage of the relational database features, such as table joins, because such a query can have a very poor performance using Local Storage.

It's easy to get started by using a very common example in most social networking apps, where there are definitions of users and memberships. You will go through a process in this recipe for the creation of an app to allow users to *subscribe* to various *groups*. This is very similar to how Facebook or Twitter may work. Here is a screenshot of the app that you will create:

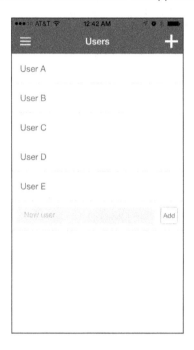

You will learn how to:

- ▸ Create a navigation menu and routes
- ▸ Add an item and save it in the SQLite database
- ▸ Update an item
- ▸ Query an item by joining multiple tables (that is, users and groups)

Getting ready

Since SQLite does not work in the browser, you have to test the app using a real mobile device or simulator.

How to do it...

Here are the instructions to create a social networking app using SQLite:

1. Start a blank project (for example, `SQLite`) and go to that folder:

```
$ ionic start SQLite blank
$ cd SQLite
```

2. Install ngCordova, as follows:

```
$ bower install ngCordova
```

3. Open `index.html` and add ngCordova in the header above `cordova.js`:

```
<script src="lib/ngCordova/dist/ng-cordova.js"></script>
```

4. Install the Cordova SQLite plugin:

```
$ cordova plugin add https://github.com/litehelpers/Cordova-
sqlite-storage.git
```

5. Change the body tag of `index.html` to the following:

```
<body ng-app="starter">
  <ion-nav-view></ion-nav-view>
</body>
```

This app will leverage the sidemenu layout. That's why you just need to start with `<ion-nav-view>`, as the rest will be injected into that directive.

6. Create a `layout.html` file and save it in the `templates` folder under www:

```
<ion-side-menus enable-menu-with-back-views="true">
  <ion-side-menu-content>
    <ion-nav-bar class="bar bar-dark">
      <ion-nav-buttons side="left">
        <button class="button button-icon icon ion-navicon"
        menu-toggle="left"></button>
      </ion-nav-buttons>
    </ion-nav-bar>

    <ion-nav-view name="main" animation="slide-left-
  right"></ion-nav-view>
  </ion-side-menu-content>

  <ion-side-menu side="left" width="150">
```

```
        <ion-content>
          <ion-list>
            <ion-item class="item" ui-sref="app.users"
            menu-close>
              Users
            </ion-item>
            <ion-item class="item" ui-sref="app.groups"
            menu-close>
              Groups
            </ion-item>
          </ion-list>
        </ion-content>
      </ion-side-menu>

    </ion-side-menus>
```

This layout will give you `<ion-nav-view>` as the content area. The menu will be on the left, with **Users** and **Groups** as two menu items.

7. The **Users** menu will let you view a list of users. If you click on a user, the app will show a modal with the groups that the user belongs to. You can save the changes in this modal and review them in the **Groups** menu. This **Groups** page is just a view-only page that provides a summary of the mapping relationship between the users and groups. So first, let's create a `users.html` template:

```
<ion-view view-title="Users">
  <ion-content>
    <ion-list>
      <ion-item class="item" ng-repeat="user in users"
      ng-click="openUserModal(user)">
        {{ user.name }}
      </ion-item>
      <div class="item item-input-inset">
        <label class="item-input-wrapper">
          <input type="text" placeholder="New user"
          ng-model="newUser.name">
        </label>
        <button class="button button-small"
        ng-click="addUser()">
          Add
        </button>
      </div>
    </ion-list>
  </ion-content>
</ion-view>
```

Note that the last line item is used to add a new user. This function is called
`adduser()`. You will write a controller for this later. Also, another function that
you should take note of is `openUserModal(user)`, which will list all the groups
the user belongs to.

8. For the user modal that shows the group list, you have to create a separate file
    called `userModal.html`:

```
<ion-modal-view>
  <ion-header-bar class="bar bar-dark">
    <button class="button button-clear"
    ng-click="cancel()">Cancel</button>
    <h1 class="title">User Detail</h1>
    <button class="button button-clear"
    ng-click="save(user, usergroup)">Save</button>
  </ion-header-bar>
  <ion-content>
    <div class="list">
      <label class="item item-checkbox" ng-repeat="group
      in groups">
        <label class="checkbox">
          <input type="checkbox"
          ng-model="usergroup[$index]">
        </label>
        {{ group.name }}
      </label>
    </div>
  </ion-content>
</ion-modal-view>
```

This modal just has the **Cancel** and **Save** buttons. The group list is just shown as
checkboxes in `ng-repeat` of the `$scope.groups` model. You will also write the
controller function to handle this later.

9. The final template is used to display the content in the **Groups** menu. Let's call
    this the `groups.html` file:

```
<ion-view view-title="Groups">
  <ion-nav-buttons side="right">
    <button class="button button-icon button-clear
    ion-plus" ng-click="openGroupModal()"></button>
  </ion-nav-buttons>
  <ion-content>
    <div class="list">
      <div ng-repeat="group in groups">
        <label class="item item-divider">
```

```
      {{ group.name }}
    </label>
    <label class="item" ng-repeat="user in
    group.users">
      {{ user.name }}
    </label>
  </div>
 </div>
 </ion-content>
</ion-view>
```

Like the group list modal, this one also lists all the groups, including the users in each group. You can get an overall view of the relationship of the group and its members. This is a view-only template, as there won't be any function to handle change or save. The purpose is to show how the SQLite query join works.

10. Now, let's move to `app.js`, where you will write the controller and services to handle all the data operations. First, you need to create the routes, as follows:

```
var app = angular.module('starter', ['ionic',
'ngCordova']);

app.config(function($stateProvider, $urlRouterProvider) {
  $stateProvider
  .state('app', {
    url: "/app",
    abstract: true,
    templateUrl: "templates/layout.html",
    controller: 'MainCtrl'
  })
    .state('app.users', {
      url: "/users",
      views: {
        'main': {
          templateUrl: "templates/users.html",
          controller: "UsersCtrl"
        }
      }
    })
    .state('app.groups', {
      url: "/groups",
      views: {
        'main': {
          templateUrl: "templates/groups.html"
```

```
      }
    }
  });

  $urlRouterProvider.otherwise('/app/users');
});
```

The routing is straightforward, as it will start with `layout.html` and replace the `<ion-nav-view name="main">` node with either `users.html` or `groups.html`, depending on the URL. Note that you need to declare ngCordova as a dependency for the app.

11. In order to handle the database, you need to create a factory to open the database, populate it with initial data, and perform data operations specifically for this app. Let's add the following to `app.js`:

```
app.factory('MyData', function($ionicPlatform,
$cordovaSQLite, $q) {
  var db = {},
      users = [],
      groups = [],
      usergroup = [];

  var initdb = {
    users: ["User A", "User B", "User C", "User D",
    "User E"],
    groups: ["Group 1", "Group 2", "Group 3"]
  };
});
```

You will use the `db` object to store the database object itself, which is basically a local file in the device filesystem. The users and groups will keep track of the existing data in the memory for **Users** and **Groups**. In order to map the relationship between them, you will use the `usergroup` array. You can change the values in `initdb`, as it's used to initialize the database with some sample datasets.

12. When the app is started, you need to create the tables (this example actually drops the previous tables to start afresh) and populate them with `initdb`:

```
var createUsers = function() {
  $cordovaSQLite.nestedExecute(db,
    'CREATE TABLE IF NOT EXISTS users (id integer primary
    key, name text)',
    'INSERT INTO users (name) VALUES (?),(?),(?),(?),(?)',
    [],
    initdb.users
```

```
       ).then(function(res) {

         $cordovaSQLite.execute(db, 'SELECT * FROM
         users').then(function(res) {

           for (var i=0; i<res.rows.length; i++) {
             users.push(res.rows.item(i));
           }

         }, function (err) {
           console.error(err);
         });

       }, function (err) {
         console.error(err);
       });
     };

     var createGroups = function() {
       $cordovaSQLite.nestedExecute(db,
         'CREATE TABLE IF NOT EXISTS groups (id integer primary
         key, name text)',
         'INSERT INTO groups (name) VALUES (?),(?),(?)',
         [],
         initdb.groups
         ).then(function(res) {

         $cordovaSQLite.execute(db, 'SELECT * FROM
         groups').then(function(res) {

           for (var i=0; i<res.rows.length; i++) {
             groups.push(res.rows.item(i));
           }

         }, function (err) {
           console.error(err);
         });

       }, function (err) {
         console.error(err);
       });
     }

     $ionicPlatform.ready(function() {
```

```
db = $cordovaSQLite.openDB("my.db", 1);

$cordovaSQLite.execute(db, 'DROP TABLE IF EXISTS
users').then(function(res) {
  createUsers();
}, function (err) {
  console.error(err);
});

$cordovaSQLite.execute(db, 'DROP TABLE IF EXISTS
groups').then(function(res) {
  createGroups();
}, function (err) {
  console.error(err);
});

$cordovaSQLite.execute(db, 'DROP TABLE IF EXISTS
usergroup').then(function(res) {
  $cordovaSQLite.execute(db, 'CREATE TABLE IF NOT EXISTS
  usergroup (id integer primary key, userId integer,
  groupId integer)').then(function(res) {
  }, function (err) {
    console.error(err);
  });

}, function (err) {
  console.error(err);
});

});
```

This initialization code must be inside the factory and not in the `return` object because we want it to be executed once the factory name is declared in the controller. This app will start afresh with no *mapping relationship* between any user and group. So, your `usergroup` table will be empty at the beginning.

13. You can continue to write the rest of the functions that handle data in the `return` `{}` function of the `MyData` factory, as follows:

```
return {
  users: users,
  groups: groups,
  getGroupsByUserId: function(userId) {
    var q = $q.defer();
    var query = "SELECT groupId FROM usergroup WHERE
    userId = (?)";
```

```
        $cordovaSQLite.execute(db, query,
        [userId]).then(function(res) {
          q.resolve(res);
        }, function (err) {
          console.error(err);
          q.reject(err);
        });

        return q.promise;
      },
      getGroupsAll: function() {
        var q = $q.defer();
        var query = "SELECT groups.id, groups.name,
        GROUP_CONCAT(usergroup.userId) AS userIds FROM groups
        LEFT OUTER JOIN usergroup ON groups.id =
        usergroup.groupId GROUP BY usergroup.groupId";
        $cordovaSQLite.execute(db, query).then(function(res) {
          q.resolve(res);
        }, function (err) {
          q.reject(err);
        });

        return q.promise;
      },
      addUser: function(params) {
        var q = $q.defer();
        var query = "INSERT INTO users (name) VALUES (?)";
        $cordovaSQLite.execute(db, query,
        [params.name]).then(function(res) {
          q.resolve(res);
        }, function (err) {
          console.error(err);
          q.reject(err);
        });

        return q.promise;
      },
    updateGroupByUserId: function(userId, usergroups) {
        var q = $q.defer();
        var query = "DELETE FROM usergroup WHERE userId = (?)";
        $cordovaSQLite.execute(db, query,
        [userId]).then(function(res) {
```

```
      var query = "INSERT INTO usergroup (userId, groupId)
      VALUES (?,?)";
      $cordovaSQLite.insertCollection(db, query,
      usergroups).then(function(res) {
        q.resolve(res);
      }, function (err) {
        console.error(err);
        q.reject(err);
      });

    }, function (err) {
      console.error(err);
      q.reject(err);
    });

    return q.promise;
  }
}
```

14. The next step is to create the `UsersCtrl` controller:

```
app.controller('UsersCtrl', function($scope, $timeout,
$ionicModal, $cordovaSQLite, MyData) {
  $scope.newUser = {};

  $ionicModal.fromTemplateUrl('templates/userModal.html', {
    scope: $scope,
    animation: 'fade-in'
  }).then(function(modal) {
    $scope.userModal = modal;
  });

  $scope.openUserModal = function(user) {
    $scope.user = user || {};
    $scope.usergroup = [];
    if ((user) && (angular.isObject(user)) &&
    (user.hasOwnProperty('id'))) {
      $scope.user.groups = [];
      MyData.getGroupsByUserId(user.id).then(function(res)
      {
        for (var i=0; i<res.rows.length; i++) {
          $scope.user.groups.push(
          res.rows.item(i).groupId);
        }
```

```
        for (var i=0; i<$scope.groups.length; i++) {
          $scope.usergroup.push(
          $scope.user.groups.indexOf(
          $scope.groups[i].id) >= 0);
        }
      });
    }

    $scope.userModal.show();
  };

  $scope.addUser = function() {
    MyData.addUser($scope.newUser.name).then(function(res) {
      $scope.users.push({
        id: res.insertId,
        name: $scope.newUser.name
      });
      $scope.newUser.name = '';
    });
  }

  $scope.save = function(user, usergroup) {
    var usergroups = [];
    for (var i=0; i<$scope.groups.length; i++) {
      if (usergroup[i]) {
        usergroups.push([user.id, $scope.groups[i].id]);
      }
    }

    MyData.updateGroupByUserId(user.id,
    usergroups).then(function(res) {
    });

    $scope.userModal.hide();
  };

  $scope.cancel = function() {
    $scope.userModal.hide();
  };

});
```

15. The following is the code that is used to handle `MainCtrl`, which tights to the `app` state. If you assign a controller to a higher-level state, it will automatically become the parent controller of its children states' controllers:

```
app.controller('MainCtrl', function($scope, $rootScope,
MyData) {
  $scope.users = MyData.users;
  $scope.groups = MyData.groups;

  $rootScope.$on('$stateChangeStart', function(event,
  toState, toParams, fromState, fromParams) {
    if (toState.name == 'app.groups') {
      getGroups();
    }
  });

  function getGroups() {
    MyData.getGroupsAll().then(function(res) {
      var newGroups = [];
      for (var i=0; i<res.rows.length; i++) {
        newGroups[i] = {
          id: res.rows.item(i).id,
          name: res.rows.item(i).name,
          users: []
        };
        var userIds = res.rows.item(i).userIds ?
        res.rows.item(i).userIds.split(',') : [];
        for (var j=0; j<userIds.length; j++) {
          var name = '';
          for (var t=0; t<$scope.users.length; t++) {
            if ($scope.users[t].id == userIds[j])
              name = $scope.users[t].name
          }
          newGroups[i].users.push({
            id: userIds[j],
            name: name
          });
        }
      }

      if (newGroups.length < $scope.groups.length) {
        for (var o=0; o<$scope.groups.length; o++) {
          var doesExist = false;
```

```
          for (var n=0; n<newGroups.length; n++) {
            doesExist = doesExist || (newGroups[n].id ==
            $scope.groups[o].id);
          }
          if (!doesExist) {
            newGroups.push({
              id: $scope.groups[o].id,
              name: $scope.groups[o].name,
              users: []
            });
          }
        }
      }
    }
    angular.copy(newGroups, $scope.groups);
  });
  }
});
```

The following two lines basically assign the *reference* pointing to the `users` and `groups` object from the `MyData` factory:

```
$scope.users = MyData.users;
$scope.groups = MyData.groups;
```

This means that if you update the data, you will always have the same data in the controller. There is no need to keep using `get()`.

16. To test the app, you must run it within a simulator or physical device.

How it works...

For SQLite to initialize properly, the initialization code must start first by checking for the `$ionicPlatform.ready` event before opening the database. This is done to avoid calling the SQLite functions when the device is still loading. If you don't want the app to start afresh with new tables each time the app runs, you can remove all the DROP TABLE queries.

To open the database for operations, you can use the following simple `openDB()` function:

```
db = $cordovaSQLite.openDB("my.db", 1);
```

This example leverages the `nestedExecute()` function to run one query after another. The `$cordovaSQLite` only gives you the ability to nest one level. For additional nesting, you have to call `$cordovaSQLite.execute()` again from within the **promise**. Unfortunately, SQLite does not give you the inserted data. So, you have to run the SELECT query after successful inserts in order to retrieve all the IDs for each row.

The `MyData` factory has several key functions to work with SQLite:

- ▶ `addUser()`: This is used to add a user. The `addUser()` function will handle data insertions.

- ▶ `getGroupsByUserId()`: When you click on a specific user, it will pop up the modal and call the `getGroupsByUserId()` function to get a list of all the groups that the user is a member of.

- ▶ `updateGroupByUserId()`: When you change the mapping relationship in the modal, `updateGroupByUserId()` will save all the changes. This update function actually deletes all the existing relationships and inserts new relationships back in the `usergroup` table. In a real-world scenario, you can optimize this process to just `REPLACE`, `INSERT`, or `DELETE`, based on the new data.

- ▶ `getGroupsAll()`: Under the **Groups** menu, you need to call `getGroupsAll()` in order to get all the groups and the members in each group. This `getGroupsAll()` is probably the most complex query in this example, because it performs a `JOIN` operation between the groups and the `usergroup` table. This is required, since you want to get the IDs as well as the names for all the groups. Also, all the user IDs will be aggregated into a string with a comma delimited using `GROUP_CONCAT`. In your controller, you can separate the user IDs again by using the `array split()` function.

The complexity within `MyData.getGroupsAll()` is due to the fact that you need to *translate* data from the query into objects. That's why you need to loop through all the rows to get the group information. Then, within each group, you get the list of `userIds` and names. Finally, if the group has no user, you need to also show it by adding back into the array.

The `UsersCtrl` controller is where you tie everything together. If you remember the input box at the end of the list, it is supposed to call `$scope.addUser()`, which will pass the name string to `MyData.addUser()`. When you click on a user, it will open a modal with `$scope.openUserModal()` and then get the group membership from `MyData.getGroupsByUserId(user.id)`. The saving action is done via `MyData.updateGroupByUserId()`:

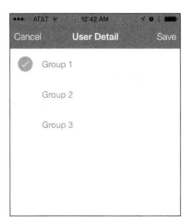

This controller assumes that the user list (`$scope.users`) and the group list (`$scope.groups`) objects are already available. Actually, these two variables are inherited from the parent `MainCtrl` controller.

Looking under the hood, the SQLite database is just a local file in the device. This means that you may need to think ahead as regards whether it should be backed up or the user is allowed to download. You need to change the second parameter, which is the location option in the following line:

```
db = $cordovaSQLite.openDB("my.db", 1);
```

However, the location option is only applicable for iOS. The following is the description for each option:

Value	Description
0 (default)	Documents that are visible to iTunes and backed up by iCloud
1	The library that is backed up by iCloud and is not visible to iTunes
2	Library/Local Database that is not visible to iTunes and not backed up by iCloud

There's more...

Other than this, SQLite behaves in a way that is very similar to that of standard SQL. The trade-off for long-term performance and storage capacity is the embedded complexity of working with the SQL queries. In addition to this, the design of SQL intends to eliminate the loss of data that may be caused due to an app crash or a power failure of the device. If you want to completely erase all the SQLite data of your app, use the `deleteDB()` function, as follows:

```
$cordovaSQLite.deleteDB("my.db");
```

See also

▶ You can find out more information about SQLite at `https://www.sqlite.org/`.

▶ Currently, the SQLite plugin does not work well with the Windows Phone. You can check out the notes in their documentation by simply navigating to `https://github.com/litehelpers/Cordova-sqlite-storage`.

5
Handling Gestures and Events

In this chapter, we will cover the following tasks related to handling gestures and events:

- ▸ Detecting drag events with a gesture coordinate
- ▸ Communication between a view, controller, and directive using events

Introduction

It's possible to write a simple app with a handful of pages. However, when the app grows, managing different views and their custom data at a specific time or a triggered event can be very complex. Ionic comes with UI-Router by default. So, you should leverage this advanced routing management mechanism. In general, the following holds true:

- ▸ A view should have its own state, which is basically a JSON object
- ▸ A route (URL) will point to a view and its assigned controller
- ▸ State and view should allow nested views so that you can manage the hierarchy

Since Ionic introduces many new components, you have to understand how those components impact your app's state hierarchy when each state is triggered.

Detecting drag events with a gesture coordinate

Most mobile UI components leverage dragging to create a better touch-and-feel experience. One common component that you will see everywhere is the scroll list. Another example is the left or right menu. That's why it's important to understand the basic mechanism of a gesture for drag events. It's even possible for you to create custom mobile components using gesture events and pure HTML/CSS/JavaScript.

In this recipe, you will build an app example to understand how to use the data from gesture events. The app will capture drag start, duration, and end events using `$ionicGesture` to give you granular coordinate data for real-time processing. In terms of the UI, you will create a `div` box to allow the dragging and showing of a coordinate.

Getting ready

Gestures can work on both web and physical devices. However, it's highly recommended to test gestures on a physical device in order to experiment with the screen size and potential performance impacts.

How to do it...

Here are the instructions to detect drag events with a gesture coordinate:

1. Create a new app using the `blank` template and go into the folder:

   ```
   $ ionic start Gesture blank
   $ cd Gesture
   ```

2. You need to set up the Sass dependencies to style the box, as follows:

   ```
   $ ionic setup sass
   ```

3. Open the `index.html` file and replace the `<body>` tag with the following code:

   ```
   <body ng-app="starter" ng-controller="MainCtrl">
     <div class="draggable" draggable="pos">
       <p>{{ pos.x }}, {{ pos.y }}<p>
     </div>
   </body>
   ```

You will write more code for `MainCtrl` later in `app.js`. The main focus here is actually the `draggable` attribute of the `div` element. This will basically allow you to bind the drag events.

4. Open `app.js` to edit it with the following code:

```
var app = angular.module('starter', ['ionic'])

app.controller('MainCtrl', function($scope) {
  $scope.pos = {
    x: 0,
    y: 0
  }
});
```

This code is used to simply initialize the `pos` object so that you can track the `x` and `y` coordinates later.

5. Now create the `draggable` directive, as follows:

```
app.directive('draggable', function($ionicGesture) {
  return {
    link: function (scope, element, attrs) {
      var elementSize = 100;

      var x = Math.round((window.screen.width -
      elementSize) / 2, 0),
          y = Math.round((window.screen.height -
          elementSize) / 2, 0);

      scope.pos.x = x;
      scope.pos.y = y;

      element[0].style[ionic.CSS.TRANSFORM] =
      'translate3d(' + x + 'px, ' + y + 'px, 0)';

      $ionicGesture.on('dragstart', function(ev) {
        console.log('dragstart: ');
        console.log(ev);
      }, element);

      $ionicGesture.on('dragend', function(ev) {
        console.log('dragend: ');
        console.log(ev);
```

```
        x += ev.gesture.deltaX;
        y += ev.gesture.deltaY;
      }, element);

      $ionicGesture.on('drag transform', function(ev) {
        console.log('drag transform: ');
        console.log(ev);

        scope.pos.x = Math.round(x + ev.gesture.deltaX, 0);
        scope.pos.y = Math.round(y + ev.gesture.deltaY, 0);
        scope.$digest();

        element[0].style[ionic.CSS.TRANSFORM] =
        'translate3d(' + (x + ev.gesture.deltaX)+ 'px, ' +
        (y + ev.gesture.deltaY) + 'px, 0)';
      }, element);

    }
  }
});
```

This directive will effectively apply to only the `div` element where it was assigned. The purpose is to detect the drag events and appropriately process the user's touch coordinate in order to move the box.

6. To style your app, add the `draggable` class in `/scss/ionic.app.scss` so that it looks like a red box with some coordinate text at the center, as follows:

```
.draggable {
  background-color: $assertive;
  color: white;
  position: absolute;
  width: 100px;
  height: 100px;
  line-height: 100px;
  vertical-align: middle;
  text-align: center;
  z-index: 20;
}
```

7. Test the app in the browser or a physical device. This is the screenshot of the app:

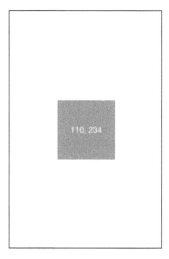

How it works...

The view and stylesheet for this app is very simple, as this is not the focus in this recipe. Let's take a look at the `draggable` directive in detail. The assumption is that this square box has a size of 100 px:

```
var elementSize = 100;
```

This must also match the `draggable` class in the `scss` file.

The core enabler that is used to detect the drag events is the `$ionicGesture.on()` function. There are three events to watch:

- ▶ `dragstart`: When the drag begins
- ▶ `drag`: During the dragging process
- ▶ `dragend`: When the drag ends

If you run this app in the browser, you can monitor the console for the outputs of these events:

```
dragstart:
 ▶ Event {gesture: Object}
drag:
 ▶ Event {gesture: Object}
drag:
 ▶ Event {gesture: Object}
drag:
 ▶ Event {gesture: Object}
drag:
 ▶ Event {gesture: Object}
dragend:
 ▶ Event {gesture: Object}
```

The `dragstart` and `dragend` events are only triggered once, while the `drag` event is continuous. It's very granular. Hence, it gives you a very smooth movement. If you expand the gesture object, which is returned from the `drag` event, you can see the detailed data:

```
drag:
 ▼ Event {gesture: Object} ⬤
    bubbles: true
    cancelBubble: false
    cancelable: true
    currentTarget: null
    defaultPrevented: false
    eventPhase: 0
  ▼ gesture: Object
      angle: 87.45519562018707
    ▶ center: Object
      deltaTime: 250
      deltaX: 0.05599386379279281
      deltaY: 1.2598619353379092
      direction: "down"
      distance: 1.2611056295552043
      eventType: "move"
      pointerType: "touch"
    ▶ preventDefault: function ()
      rotation: 0
      scale: 1
    ▶ srcEvent: TouchEvent
    ▶ startEvent: Object
    ▶ stopDetect: function ()
    ▶ stopPropagation: function ()
    ▶ target: p.ng-binding
      timeStamp: 1439260009223
    ▶ touches: TouchList
      velocityX: 0.00022397545517117124
      velocityY: 0.005039447741351637
    ▶ __proto__: Object
  ▶ path: Array[6]
    returnValue: true
  ▶ srcElement: p.ng-binding
  ▶ target: p.ng-binding
    timeStamp: 1439260009225
    type: "drag"
  ▶ __proto__: Event
```

There are many types of data available for you to use such as target element, angle, timestamp, direction, and so on. However, your main interest here is to use the `deltaX` and `deltaY` to detect the new position of the touch pointer. The delta values are a measure of how far it is from the original position when the dragging started.

To use the delta values, you just need to change the `pos.x` and `pos.y` values of the scope by adding the delta value for the *x* and *y* coordinate, as follows:

```
scope.pos.x = Math.round(x + ev.gesture.deltaX, 0);
scope.pos.y = Math.round(y + ev.gesture.deltaY, 0);
scope.$digest();
```

Keep in mind that you must call the `$digest()` function for the AngularJS digest cycle to kick in. The reason behind this is that `$ionicGesture.on()` will not do this for us, as it's outside the default AngularJS controller, directive, or service.

The final part is to apply the new coordinate to the box by changing its transform value, as follows:

```
element[0].style[ionic.CSS.TRANSFORM] = 'translate3d(' + (x +
ev.gesture.deltaX)+ 'px, ' + (y + ev.gesture.deltaY) + 'px, 0)';
```

There obviously are many ways to execute the actual animation. However, using a CSS Transform always gives a better performance and frame rate. Again, `element[0]` is the `div` object that you applied this directive on.

When the drag is performed, you just need to save the new position, as follows:

```
x += ev.gesture.deltaX;
y += ev.gesture.deltaY;
```

See also

It's possible to implement velocity with the help of `velocityX` and `velocityY` when the `drag` event ends. This will allow your object to continue the motion after the touch has completed.

- ▸ Ionic has some default directives to handle gestures such as on-drag-left, on-drag-right, and so on, which can be found at `http://ionicframework.com/docs/api/directive/onHold/`.

- ▸ However, you may not get the flexibility and rich set of data from $ionicGesture: `http://ionicframework.com/docs/api/service/$ionicGesture/`. This is because the default directives hid away the granularity of `$ionicGesture`. For example, you cannot access coordinate data.

Communication between a view, controller, and directive using events

One of the most confusing aspects of using Ionic is when and how to leverage eventing for communication between various components. Let's take a look at the various scenarios and different ways to handle the data flow:

- **State to view and/or controller**: This is handled by UI-Router. There are several options. You can use the `resolve` object declared at the route level and pass it to the controller just as a factory. Another option is to pass data as a parameter in `$stateParams` so that the controller for that specific state can receive data.

- **View to view**: To share data in different views, store them in a parent scope, `$stateParams`, or factory. If it's just a simple piece of data, mainly for display purposes, it's OK to use the parent scope method. However, if the data is specific to state, it should be a part of the state parameters. Factory is always a good practice to keep the shared data between state, view, and controller. You just have to write the getter and setter methods for the factory.

- **View to controller**: Communication is done via the two-way binding of the `$scope` variables.

- **Controller to controller**: The data can be passed from the parent to child `$scope`, sent via some type of $broadcast event or detected from model change using `$watch`. The example in this section will go over these mechanisms.

- **Controller to directive**: There are two options here. You can watch the model change from within the directive. This gives you the ability to get an old and a new value. Alternatively, you can pass the model directly to the directive without creating an isolated scope. This directive will use this model with the same reference to the scope model.

- **Factory to factory**: For internal communication between factories and services, you just need to declare the factory in the function parameters just as a controller.

- **Directive to factory**: There is normally no need to communicate between a directive and factory. The reason is that your controller should take care as a middle man in this process.

The app example in this recipe will explain how to broadcast an event and watch for a variable change in a controller and directive. In addition, you will have some fun exploring the two types of horizontal scrolling, which are commonly used in many mobile apps.

The following is the screenshot of the app that you will build:

Getting ready

Since AngularJS and UI-Router comes with the Ionic bundle, there is no need to prepare this in a physical device.

How to do it...

Here are the instructions to enable communication among a view, controller, and directive using events:

1. Create a new app using the `blank` template and go into the respective folder, as follows:

    ```
    $ ionic start HorizontalSlide blank
    $ cd HorizontalSlide
    ```

2. You need to set up the Sass dependencies because you will create a horizontal scroll class later:

    ```
    $ ionic setup sass
    ```

3. Open the `index.html` file and replace the `<body>` tag with the following:

```
<body ng-app="starter" ng-controller="MainCtrl">
  <ion-pane>
    <ion-header-bar class="bar-stable">
      <h1 class="title">Events</h1>
    </ion-header-bar>
    <ion-content scroll="false">

    </ion-content>
  </ion-pane>
</body>
```

This is just a skeleton of the app view. You will fill out three more sections within `<ion-content>` later.

4. The first section of the view is for the free-style horizontal scroller:

```
<div class="item item-divider">
  Free Scroll
  <span class="item-note">
    More
  </span>
</div>

<ion-scroll direction="x" class="horizontal-scroll
padding" ng-controller="FirstCtrl">
  <button class="button button-positive button-large"
  ng-click="broadcast('Ionic')">
    <i class="icon ion-ionic"></i>
  </button>
  <button class="button button-calm button-large"
  ng-click="broadcast('Twitter')">
    <i class="icon ion-social-twitter"></i>
  </button>
  <button class="button button-balanced button-large"
  ng-click="broadcast('Facebook')">
    <i class="icon ion-social-facebook"></i>
  </button>
  <button class="button button-energized button-large"
  ng-click="broadcast('Googleplus')">
    <i class="icon ion-social-googleplus"></i>
  </button>
  <button class="button button-assertive button-large"
  ng-click="broadcast('Dribbble')">
    <i class="icon ion-social-dribbble"></i>
  </button>
```

```
  <button class="button button-royal button-large"
  ng-click="broadcast('Octocat')">
    <i class="icon ion-social-octocat"></i>
  </button>
  <button class="button button-dark button-large"
  ng-click="broadcast('Instagram')">
    <i class="icon ion-social-instagram"></i>
  </button>
</ion-scroll>
```

This `<ion-scroll>` tag will lock the scroll in the x direction only. Otherwise, it behaves just like a regular vertical scroll.

5. The second section is for the slider-style scroll:

```
<div class="item item-divider">
  Slide-by-Slide Scroll
  <span class="item-note">
    More
  </span>
</div>

<div ng-controller="SecondCtrl">
  <ion-slide-box show-pager="false">
    <ion-slide class="padding">
      <button class="button button-block
      button-positive" ng-click="changeMyData('POSITIVE')">
        POSITIVE
      </button>
    </ion-slide>
    <ion-slide class="padding">
      <button class="button button-block button-calm"
      ng-click="changeMyData('CALM')">
        CALM
      </button>
    </ion-slide>
    <ion-slide class="padding">
      <button class="button button-block button-balanced"
      ng-click="changeMyData('BALANCED')">
        BALANCED
      </button>
    </ion-slide>
  </ion-slide-box>
</div>
```

The main difference here is that the scrolling here takes place slide-by-slide, and each slide will take the full width of the screen. Once you slide to the left, it will lock or snap to the second screen.

6. The third section is just for us to view the event and variable. You will see a detailed explanation on this later on:

```
<div class="item item-divider">
  Logs
</div>

<div ng-controller="ThirdCtrl">
  <ul class="list">
    <li class="item">
      <b>myEvent </b> {{ display.value }}
    </li>
    <li class="item">
      <b>myData </b> <my-directive data="myData">
      </my-directive>
    </li>
  </ul>
</div>
```

7. Open `app.js` and insert the following code in it:

```
var app = angular.module('starter', ['ionic']);

app.controller('MainCtrl', function($scope) {
  $scope.myData = {
    value: 'No value yet'
  }

  $scope.display = {
    value: 'Not fired yet'
  }
});
```

`MainCtrl` is the parent controller, which initialized two objects (`myData` and `display`) for usage within its children controllers.

8. Let's write the three controllers that are needed to handle its three sections in the view earlier:

```
app.controller('FirstCtrl', function($scope, $rootScope) {

  $scope.broadcast = function(param) {
```

```
      $rootScope.$broadcast('myEvent', param);
    }

});

app.controller('SecondCtrl', function($scope, $rootScope) {

  $scope.changeMyData = function(param) {
    $scope.myData.value = param;
  }

});

app.controller('ThirdCtrl', function($scope, $rootScope) {

  $rootScope.$on('myEvent', function(e, val) {
    $scope.display.value = 'Fired with param: ' + val;
  });

});
```

Note that the purpose here is to understand the communication between the three controllers. So, this example is very simple, as it only triggers an event or changes some value. The third controller is your log screen, where you can view what is being changed by detecting the event.

9. Now, you can put together a directive just to test the ability to watch a model change from within the directive:

```
app.directive('myDirective', function($rootScope) {
  console.log('Start directive');
  return {
    template: '{{ myData.value }}',
    scope: {myData : '=data'},
    link: function(scope, element, attrs) {

      scope.$watch(attrs.data, function(newVal, oldVal) {
        if (newVal != oldVal) {
          console.log('myData has changed');
          console.log(newVal);
        }
      }, true);
    }
  }
});
```

This directive does not show up anywhere in the view, as it is just for you to understand the mechanism behind the scene.

10. Finally, add the `scroll` class to the first horizontal scroll in `/scss/ionic.app.scss`, as follows:

```
.horizontal-scroll {
  white-space: nowrap;
  overflow: scroll;
}
```

11. That's it. Now, you can run the app in the browser to test it.

How it works...

If you click on any button in the first scroll section, you will see that the log will show the new `myEvent` object, as shown in the following screenshot:

```
Logs

myEvent Fired with param: Ionic
```

This is because the first controller has `broadcast()` that triggers `$rootScope.$broadcast()`. You can pass a parameter to this broadcast mechanism as a way to share data. Then, in the third controller, you will see the usage of `$rootScope.$on('myEvent', function(e, val) {})`, as this will listen for `myEvent` specifically, and pass the `val` variable as the parameter value.

There are three things that you should make a note of here:

▸ You can give the event any name you like. It doesn't matter.

▸ You can pass more than one parameter. If you have two or more parameters, just go ahead and add more in the `$on()` function, such as `function(e, val1, val2,…)`.

▸ This must be done on `$rootScope`. Basically, firing an event will *stick* to a specific scope. If you fire an event at the current `$scope` object, the external `$scope` object won't be able to listen to or access the event.

In summary, you use `$broadcast` to broadcast an event, and listen by using `$on` at the `$rootScope` level. Broadcasting is a very useful and easy-to-use mechanism for the communication and sharing of data. However, you should not use broadcast everywhere. The reason behind this is that when your app scales, it's very hard to keep track of and debug all the events being broadcast. Any controller can broadcast and create a new event. You might end up creating duplicate events, or listening to multiple events for the same purpose.

Now, let's evaluate the second scenario using $watch. As you know, the AngularJS digest cycle is very important if you want to keep track of variable changes. So, when a controller function changes a variable, it will trigger $watch on that variable to execute a function. That's why you are able to see the console output of this code when you click on the **POSITIVE** button:

```
scope.$watch(attrs.data, function(newVal, oldVal) {
  if (newVal != oldVal) {
    console.log('myData has changed');
    console.log(newVal);
  }
}, true);
```

This is the output that will show up:

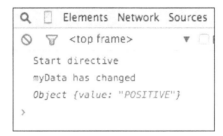

Note that the third parameter is `true`, which means that $watch will perform a deep comparison of the object. Otherwise, it will only watch a variable by default and not each key/value inside the object.

In the `myDirective` directive, there is a template with the following string:

```
{{ myData.value }}
```

This tells the view to parse the value here whenever there is a change. This `myData` object is basically brought in by the directive via the following command:

```
scope: {myData : '=data'}
```

Furthermore, if you look at the view declaration, you put an attribute called `data` to reference to the `myData` object of the controller:

```
<my-directive data="myData"></my-directive>
```

The result is the following screen update:

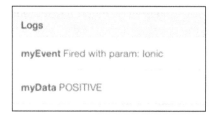

Now, `myData` shows `POSITIVE` as the string in its value key.

Although there are several steps being described here, the concept is that in order to share data from a controller to a directive, you can pass it via the attribute of that directive. Then, you bring it in via the scope declaration of the directive. The rest of the step is similar to how you handle the scope data.

See also

The best official documentation about `$broadcast` and `$watch` is the AngularJS website itself. To have a look at it, visit `https://docs.angularjs.org/api/ng/type/$rootScope.Scope`.

You should try to understand more about the detailed mechanism behind `$rootScope` in this case.

6
App Theme Customization

In this chapter, we will cover the following tasks related to theme customization:

- ▶ Customizing themes for specific platforms
- ▶ Creating an introduction screen with a custom header

Introduction

Although Ionic has its own default out-of-the-box themes, you might want to customize your app's look and feel further. There are several methods that can be used to accomplish this. The following are two of these:

- ▶ Change the stylesheet within the Sass file
- ▶ Detect a platform specific to JavaScript and apply custom classes or AngularJS conditions

Either of the aforementioned methods should work, but it's highly recommended that you apply customizations in the Sass file before the app is built in order to achieve maximum rendering performance.

In this chapter, you will create the following three sample authentication apps:

- ▶ Email and password authentication using Firebase
- ▶ Social authentication (Facebook, Twitter, and Google+) using Firebase
- ▶ Social authentication (LinkedIn) using Auth0 and Firebase

Depending on the app, you may not need to use all of these authentication methods. For example, for an app focusing on working professionals, it would make more sense to use a LinkedIn authentication to narrow down the audiences who fit the user profile of the app.

Customizing themes for specific platforms

Each mobile platform vendor has its own design guideline. This recipe will go over an example of how to address the app theme differently for iOS and Android. In traditional development, using either a native language or other hybrid app solutions, you have to keep separate repositories for each platform in order to customize the theme. This can be very inefficient in the long run.

Ionic makes it very convenient by separating the stylesheet for each platform and specific OS version within the same platform. The example in this recipe covers two possibilities of customization using Sass and JavaScript. The following screenshot shows both the iOS and Android app with different title bar colors and text:

Getting ready

There is no need to test the theme on a physical device because Ionic can render both iOS and Android in the browser.

How to do it...

Here are the instructions to customize themes for specific platforms:

1. Create a new app using the blank template and go into the respective folder:

```
$ ionic start Theme blank
$ cd Theme
```

2. You need to set up the Sass dependencies in the following way, because Ionic uses a number of external libraries for this:

```
$ ionic setup sass
```

3. Open the `index.html` file and replace the `<body>` tag with the following:

```
<body ng-app="starter" ng-controller="MainCtrl">
  <ion-pane>
    <ion-header-bar class="bar-assertive">
      <h1 class="title" ng-if="isIOS">Welcome iOS</h1>
      <h1 class="title title-left"
      ng-if="isAndroid">Welcome Android</h1>
    </ion-header-bar>
    <ion-content>
    </ion-content>
  </ion-pane>
</body>
```

You will create the `MainCtrl` controller later in `app.js` to handle platform-specific variables (such as `isIOS` and `isAndroid`).

4. Open `app.js` and add the controller, as follows:

```
.controller('MainCtrl', function($scope) {
  $scope.isIOS = ionic.Platform.isIOS();
  $scope.isAndroid = ionic.Platform.isAndroid();
});
```

5. Open the `ionic.app.scss` file under `./scss` and add the following code at the end after `@import "www/lib/ionic/scss/ionic"`:

```
.platform-android {
  .bar {
    background-color: white!important;
  }

  .bar .title {
    color: $assertive!important;
  }
}
```

This simply overrides the Android theme with a customized bar and title classes.

 This `.scss` file is in the `scss` folder in your root project. You don't want to directly modify the default `.scss` files of Ionic under `./www/lib/ionic/scss`, because it's not a good practice.

6. Conduct a test run of the app in the browser, as follows:

```
$ ionic serve --lab
```

7. If you inspect the DOM, you will see that Android-specific classes are injected into the DOM:

```
Q  🔲  | Elements | Network  Sources  Timeline  Profiles  Resources  Audits  Console  AngularJS
    ▶ <head>…</head>
    ▼ <body ng-app="starter" ng-controller="MainCtrl" class="grade-a platform-browser platform-android platform-ready">
      ▼ <ion-pane class="pane">
        ▼ <ion-header-bar class="bar-assertive bar bar-header disable-user-behavior">
            <!-- ngIf: isIOS -->
            <!-- ngIf: isAndroid -->
            <h1 class="title title-left" ng-if="isAndroid">Welcome Android</h1>
            <!-- end ngIf: isAndroid -->
          </ion-header-bar>
        ▶ <ion-content class="scroll-content ionic-scroll  has-header">…</ion-content>
        </ion-pane>
        <script>
```

How it works...

Ionic automatically created platform-specific parent classes and put them at the `<body>` tag. The iOS app will include the `.platform-ios` class. The Android app will have `.platform-android4_4` for Android v4.4, `.platform-android5_0` for Android v5.0, or just `.platform-android`. So, for stylesheet customization, you can leverage these existing classes to change the look and feel of your app.

The example also leverages an existing function in an `ionic` object to detect platforms:

```
$scope.isIOS = ionic.Platform.isIOS();
$scope.isAndroid = ionic.Platform.isAndroid();
```

By making the scope variables available to the view, you can use it to hide or show a specific DOM using `ng-if`. It's recommended that you use `ng-if` instead of `ng-show` because `ng-show` may show and hide the element right away, thus creating a *flickering* effect.

There's more...

It would be better if you could take a look at several `.scss` files under `./www/lib/ionic/scss` to understand how Ionic builds its own `.css` files. Each component has its own `.scss` file. The `_variables.scss` file will give you all the global theme variables that you can override in `./scss/ionic.app.scss`.

See also

▶ There is other device information available from the `ionic.Platform` object. You can even detect iPad devices. For more information, visit `http://ionicframework.com/docs/api/utility/ionic.Platform/`.

▸ The Ionic website also has some basic instructions on how to write a Sass theme. For more information on this, visit `http://learn.ionicframework.com/formulas/working-with-sass/`.

Creating an introduction screen with a custom header

Every app has a different onboarding experience. Some will show a short video, while others walk the users through a few introduction slides. Creating slides is useful because you can pitch initial key messages to set an expectation for users. Also, they can move between slides at their own pace. Most apps will have three to five slides for an introduction screen.

In this recipe, you will learn how to create a three-slide intro screen using `<ion-slide-box>`, which is an Ionic directive that is used to create horizontal slides. In addition to this, you will incorporate ngStorage to detect whether the user has seen the introduction or not. This is useful when you don't want users to keep seeing the introduction every time the app starts. Here is the screenshot of the app:

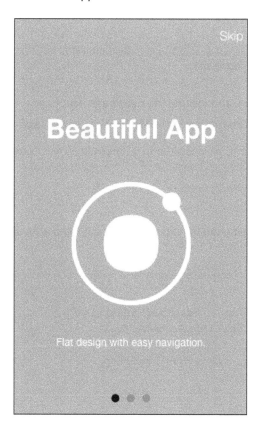

Getting ready

Since ngStorage can work locally in the browser, there is no need to test this app on a physical device.

How to do it...

Here are the instructions to create an introduction screen with custom header:

1. Create a new app using the blank template and go into the folder:

   ```
   $ ionic start Intro blank
   $ cd Intro
   ```

2. Set up the Sass dependencies, as follows:

   ```
   $ ionic setup sass
   ```

3. Install ngStorage by executing the following command:

   ```
   $ bower install ngstorage
   ```

    `ngstorage` is in lowercase in the command because ngStorage is a different repository.

4. Open `index.html` and include the ngStorage script:

   ```
   <script src="lib/ngstorage/ngStorage.js"></script>
   ```

5. For the body content, all you need to do is place a *view holder*, as follows:

   ```
   <body ng-app="starter">
     <ion-nav-view></ion-nav-view>
   </body>
   ```

   This is basically just used to hold the additional templates of the intro and app screen.

6. First, let's knock off the easy template—`app.html` in the `./www/templates` folder:

   ```
   <ion-pane>
    <ion-header-bar class="bar-assertive">
      <h1 class="title">Welcome</h1>
    </ion-header-bar>
    <ion-content class="has-header">
         Hello World!
    </ion-content>
   </ion-pane>
   ```

This template is just the app screen that you want the user to go to after viewing the introduction. Since this is not the focus of this example, you can make it super simple.

7. Create `intro.html` in the `templates` folder under `./www`, as follows:

```html
<ion-nav-view class="intro">
  <ion-header-bar align-title="middle" class="bar-balanced
  bar">
    <button class="button button-icon icon
    ion-ios-arrow-back" ng-if="slides.currentSlide > 0"
    ng-click="slides.currentSlide = slides.currentSlide-1">
    </button>
    <span class="title" ng-bind-html="title"></span>
    <button class="button button-clear" ui-sref="app">
      Skip
    </button>
  </ion-header-bar>
  <ion-content class="has-footer" scroll="false">
    <ion-slide-box active-slide="slides.currentSlide"
    on-slide-changed="slideChanged(index)">
      <ion-slide class="center">
        <div class="row">
          <div class="col">
            <h1>Beautiful App</h1>
            <div class="center-image">
              <i class="icon ion-ionic"></i>
            </div>
            <p>Flat design with easy navigation.</p>
          </div>
        </div>
      </ion-slide>
      <ion-slide class="center">
        <div class="row">
          <div class="col">
            <h1>Useful Content</h1>
            <div class="center-image">
              <i class="icon ion-ios-paper"></i>
            </div>
            <p>Daily update content for your needs.</p>
          </div>
        </div>
      </ion-slide>
      <ion-slide class="center">
        <div class="row">
```

```
        <div class="col">
          <h1>Lowest Price</h1>
          <div class="center-image">
            <i class="icon ion-social-usd"></i>
          </div>
          <p>Beat all competitor offerings.</p>
        </div>
      </div>
    </ion-slide>
  </ion-slide-box>
</ion-content>
<ion-footer-bar align-title="center" class="bar-balanced
darker-balanced" ui-sref="app" ng-if="slides.currentSlide
== 2">
  <span class="title">Get Started</span>
</ion-footer-bar>
</ion-nav-view>
```

Your intro screen is actually very simple. It has a header bar and content area.
Within the content area, you will use <ion-slide-box> to display the sliders.

8. To create the logic as regards whether to show the intro screen, you have to write
   this component when the app runs. Edit app.js in the following way:

```
var app = angular.module('starter', ['ionic',
'ngStorage']);

app.run(function($ionicPlatform, $rootScope, $state,
$localStorage) {
  $ionicPlatform.ready(function() {
    $rootScope.$storage = $localStorage.$default({
      seenIntro: false
    });

    if ($rootScope.$storage.seenIntro) {
      event.preventDefault();
      $state.go('app');
    }
  });
});
```

ngStorage is the key here because it allows you to detect `$rootScope.$storage.seenIntro` even when the app restarts.

9. Next, you need to set up the routing for the app, as follows:

```
.config(function($stateProvider, $urlRouterProvider) {

  $stateProvider

  .state('intro', {
    url: "/",
    templateUrl: "templates/intro.html",
    controller: 'IntroCtrl'
  })

  .state('app', {
    url: "/app",
    templateUrl: "templates/app.html"
  });

  $urlRouterProvider.otherwise('/');
})
```

As mentioned earlier, `intro.html` is your `intro` template with route /, while `app.html` is the main app route /app.

10. There is no need to handle anything for the app controller, but you need to do a custom title and create a `slideChanged()` function, as follows:

```
.controller('IntroCtrl', function($scope, $rootScope) {
  $scope.slides = {
    currentSlide: 0
  };
  $scope.title = '<i class="icon ion-android-home"></i>';

  $scope.slideChanged = function(index) {
    $scope.slideIndex = index;
    if (index == 2)
      $rootScope.$storage.seenIntro = true;
  };
});
```

When the user is on the last slide (when the index is 2), you set `$rootScope.$storage.seenIntro` to `true`, which indicates that the user has seen the entire intro screen.

11. Now, the critical part is to update the `ionic.app.scss` file under `./scss` to apply proper styling for the introductory screen. Let's start with the button in the last screen:

```
$balanced-darker: darken($balanced, 10%) !default;

.darker-balanced {
  background: $balanced-darker !important;
}
```

Basically, `$balanced-darker` is a darker color, which is created using the `$balanced` variable in Ionic.

12. Since the entire `intro` template has a `.intro` class, you can style all the child elements independently, as follows:

```
.intro, .intro .scroll-content {
  background-color: $balanced!important;
}

.intro .scroll, .intro .slider {
  height: 100%!important;
  background-color: $balanced;
}

.intro .center {
  display: -webkit-box;
  display: -moz-box;
  display: -ms-flexbox;
  display: -webkit-flex;
  display: flex;
  -webkit-box-direction: normal;
  -moz-box-direction: normal;
  -webkit-box-orient: horizontal;
  -moz-box-orient: horizontal;
  -webkit-flex-direction: row;
  -ms-flex-direction: row;
  flex-direction: row;
```

```
    -webkit-flex-wrap: nowrap;
    -ms-flex-wrap: nowrap;
    flex-wrap: nowrap;
    -webkit-box-pack: center;
    -moz-box-pack: center;
    -webkit-justify-content: center;
    -ms-flex-pack: center;
    justify-content: center;
    -webkit-align-content: stretch;
    -ms-flex-line-pack: stretch;
    align-content: stretch;
    -webkit-box-align: center;
    -moz-box-align: center;
    -webkit-align-items: center;
    -ms-flex-align: center;
    align-items: center;
}

.intro .center-image {
  text-align:center;
}

.intro .center-image i {
  font-size: 200px;
  color: white;
}

.intro h1, .intro p {
  color: white;
  text-align: center;
  padding: 20px 0 20px 0;
}

.intro h1 {
  font-weight: bold;
}
```

13. It's time to test the app in the browser:

```
$ ionic serve
```

14. If you go to the last screen, the button will show up. In addition to this, the back button to the top left will only be shown when there is a slide before the current one that you can go to:

How it works...

This app has several *moving parts* that you have to connect together:

- ▸ A Local Storage's `seenIntro` variable will be checked each time the app starts. Since `run()` will be executed first, you have to place the check logic there. The `$localStorage.$default()` function is used to set the default value if the variable doesn't exist yet.

- ▸ The `view-title` does not take HTML code. So, you have to place a scope variable at `<span class="title" ng-bind-html="title"></span>` to update.

- ▸ It's important to keep track of the current slide when the slide is changed by using `active-slide="slides.currentSlide"`. Once the slide is changed it will trigger an event, which can be assigned to a directive called **on-slide-changed**.

- ▸ In order to show or hide the **Back** button, you just need to check whether the current slide index is greater than zero by using `ng-if="slides.currentSlide > 0"`.

- ▸ In your footer, it's basically a button that can be used to go to the `app` state and only show whether the current slide index is two: `<ion-footer-bar align-title="center" class="bar-balanced darker-balanced" ui-sref="app" ng-if="slides.currentSlide == 2">`.

It's good practice to not change Ionic classes directly, but create a parent class for the page. In this case, you created an `intro` class so that you can modify everything in that page specifically. The Ionic slider does not *stretch* vertically by default. That's why you need to apply its height as 100%.

All the other elements within a specific slide can be customized as you wish. Normally, it's good enough to keep things simple, with a header text as your value proposition and an image and a short one-liner to explain the idea.

7

Extending Ionic with Your Own Components

In this chapter, we will cover the following tasks related to creating custom directives and filters:

- ► Creating a scroll progress bar directive
- ► Creating a custom filter
- ► Animating an app using `requestAnimationFrame` with event binding

Introduction

Although Ionic has many out-of-the-box components, you may want to start customizing the existing components or create your own. There are many scenarios where you just cannot fit the default components in your specific use cases. Here are some of the examples of the scenarios:

- ► Custom input fields
- ► The formatting of data with your specific requirements
- ► The binding of your own UI component with Ionic events
- ► The creation of animation based on stateful events

Alternatively, you can reuse the AngularJS Bootstrap module and just change its CSS to create a consistent look and feel. Since you can leverage web technologies, creating new components in Ionic is very simple. It's the same process as building new directives and filters for the AngularJS Single-Page Application. If you are unfamiliar with this, you can start with the following sections and go through some simple examples.

You will learn the following in this chapter:

- ▶ How to create custom directives and filters
- ▶ How to look for Ionic events and bind them to create stateful animation

Creating a scroll progress bar directive

Progress bars are very useful, as they indicate the amount of task that is completed. It gives users a great experience in terms of what to expect (or how long the process should take to finish). In content websites such as blogs, you may have observed that the progress bar is also used to show how much the users have read. In this recipe, you will create a custom directive to show the reading progress. The concept is very simple. This directive basically checks against the scroll position of `<ion-content>` in order to adjust the bar (`div`) length.

The following is the screenshot of the app:

There are 100 items in the list. As you scroll, the bar at the top will move from left to right to indicate the percentage of reading completed.

Getting ready

This app example can work either in a browser or physical device.

How to do it...

Here are the instructions to create a scroll progressive bar directive:

1. Create a new app using a *blank* template and go into the folder:

   ```
   $ ionic start ScrollProgress blank
   $ cd ScrollProgress
   ```

2. Set up the Sass dependencies for the custom progress bar div, as follows:

   ```
   $ ionic setup sass
   ```

3. Open the index.html file and replace the <body> tag with the following:

   ```
   <body ng-app="starter" ng-controller="MyCtrl">

     <ion-header-bar class="bar-positive">
       <h1 class="title">Reading List</h1>
       <scroll-progress></scroll-progress>
     </ion-header-bar>

     <ion-content>
       <ion-list>
         <ion-item ng-repeat="item in items">
           Item {{ item.id }}
         </ion-item>
       </ion-list>
     </ion-content>

   </body>
   ```

   There is nothing special about the view structure. What you have here is just a header bar and a list of items. However, there is a new scroll-progress directive to indicate the scroll progress of the list.

4. Open app.js to edit it with the following code:

   ```
   var app = angular.module('starter', ['ionic']);

   app.controller('MyCtrl', function($scope, $ionicScrollDelegate) {

     $scope.items = [];
   ```

```
     for (var i=1; i<=100; i++) {
       $scope.items.push({ id: i });
     }

});
```

Again, to simplify the unimportant part, this `MyCtrl` controller will just populate the list with 100 items.

5. To create the custom scroll progress directive, you need to add the following code:

```
app.directive('scrollProgress',
function($ionicScrollDelegate) {
   return {
      template: '<div class="progress"
      style=\'{{percentage}}\'></div>',
      link: function (scope, element, attrs) {
        scope.percentage = '0%';

        ionic.DomUtil.ready(function() {
          var windowHeight = $ionicScrollDelegate.
          _instances[0].element.clientHeight,
             scrollHeight = $ionicScrollDelegate.
             _instances[0].element.querySelector(
             'div.scroll').clientHeight,
             delta = scrollHeight - windowHeight;

          $ionicScrollDelegate._instances[0].
          $element.bind('scroll', function(e) {
            var scrollPosition = $ionicScrollDelegate.
            getScrollPosition().top;
            scope.percentage = 'width:
            ' + (scrollPosition / delta * 100) + '%';
            scope.$digest();
          });
        });
      }
   };
});
```

This custom directive will use `$ionicScrollDelegate`, which is a standard out-of-the-box delegate from Ionic that is used to get and set the position of the scroller.

6. Finally, just add the styling for the `progress` class in `ionic.app.scss`, as follows:

```scss
.progress {
  height: 3px;
  background: darken(#33cd5f, 70%);
  position:absolute;
  left: 0;
  bottom: 0;
}
```

How it works...

The progress bar is just a `div` element with the width as a percentage. It must be a part of the header, as it is positioned between the header and the main content.

It's important to understand how Ionic structures its content and scroll element. In order to access the information of these elements, you need to work through `$ionicScrollDelegate`. There are four variables that can be used to calculate the percentage:

```javascript
var windowHeight = $ionicScrollDelegate.
_instances[0].element.clientHeight,
    scrollHeight = $ionicScrollDelegate._instances[0]
    .element.querySelector('div.scroll').clientHeight,
    delta = scrollHeight - windowHeight;
```

This also can be used:

```javascript
var scrollPosition =
$ionicScrollDelegate.getScrollPosition().top;
```

The `windowHeight` variable is the height of the device screen or the visible content area. The `scrollHeight` variable is the real height of the scrollable element (`div.scroll`). So, when you scroll, this element will change its top position to simulate the scrolling effect. The delta variable is used to calculate the percentage. By default, you will see the first screen. So, you need to subtract the height of the screen to get your starting point. The `scrollPosition` variable is the top position of `div.scroll`, and this variable is updated every time the binding to the `scroll` event is triggered.

One tricky part that you should be aware of is the difference between element and `$element`. Here's the `element` part:

```javascript
$ionicScrollDelegate._instances[0].element
```

Here's the $element part:

```
$ionicScrollDelegate._instances[0].$element
```

This is an undocumented area, which requires you to carefully inspect in the console before using. Eventually, any <ion-content> directive will create a $ionicScrollDelegate._ instances[0] instance in its delegate. You can look at the values of this object to find out the difference between element and $element:

```
▼ Object {_scrollViewOptions: Object, element: ion-content.top-image.scroll-content.ionic-scroll.has-header,
    $$delegateHandle: undefined
  ▶ $$filterFn: function ()
  ▼ $element: JQLite[1]
    ▶ 0: ion-content.top-image.scroll-content.ionic-scroll.has-header
      length: 1
    ▶ __proto__: Object[0]
  ▶ __timeout: function timeout(fn, delay, invokeApply)
  ▶ _scrollViewOptions: Object
  ▶ _setRefresher: function (refresherScope, refresherElement, refresherMethods)
  ▶ anchorScroll: function (shouldAnimate)
  ▼ element: ion-content.top-image.scroll-content.ionic-scroll.has-header
      accessKey: ""
    ▶ attributes: NamedNodeMap
      baseURI: "http://localhost:8100/"
      childElementCount: 2
    ▶ childNodes: NodeList[2]
    ▶ children: HTMLCollection[2]
    ▶ classList: DOMTokenList[4]
      className: "top-image scroll-content ionic-scroll has-header"
      clientHeight: 526
      clientLeft: 0
      clientTop: 0
      clientWidth: 320
      contentEditable: "inherit"
    ▶ dataset: DOMStringMap
      dir: ""
      draggable: false
    ▶ firstChild: div.scroll
    ▶ firstElementChild: div.scroll
      hidden: false
      id: ""
      innerHTML: "<div class="scroll" style="transform: translate3d(0px, 0px, 0px) scale(1);">⤶ <ion-list cl
      innerText: "Item 1⤶Item 2⤶Item 3⤶Item 4⤶Item 5⤶Item 6⤶Item 7⤶Item 8⤶Item 9⤶Item 10⤶Item 11⤶Item 12⤶Ite
```

Basically, the element property is the actual DOM element, while $element is an AngularJS version (or JQLite) of this. You can use element to get the DOM properties such as height and width. However, the scroll binding is only available in $element, as it is a specific functionality of Ionic.

When you create a custom directive, you can insert your own template within that directive, as follows:

```
template: '<div class="progress" style=\'{{percentage}}\'></div>'
```

In this case, the `percentage` variable will be interpolated into the style attribute of this `div` element.

Whenever you are interacting with the out-of-the-box elements of Ionic, you need to make sure that they are rendered completely by putting your code within the `ionic.DomUtil.ready` event. In addition to this, the `bind()` function will not trigger the AngularJS scope digest cycle. That's why you need to call `scope.$digest()` manually within the scroll binding. This is the only way AngularJS knows how to look for changes and update the view with your new `percentage` value.

See also

For more information about creating a custom directive, check out the AngularJS documentation for directives by visiting `https://docs.angularjs.org/guide/directive`.

Creating a custom filter

Filters are a feature of AngularJS and not specific to Ionic. The main reason you might want to use a filter is when you just need the data to be displayed in a different format in the view. You don't want to change the actual value in the controller or factory. This makes things very convenient because you don't have to decide upon a specific format within the controller code while leaving the flexibility in the view component.

Here is the list of some out-of-the-box filters (from `https://docs.angularjs.org/api/ng/filter`):

- `currency`
- `number`
- `date`
- `json`
- `lowercase`
- `uppercase`
- `limitTo`
- `orderBy`

In this recipe, you will learn how to add more filters using the `angular-filter` module as well as create a custom filter. The following is the screenshot of the app:

Getting ready

There is no need to test in a physical device because the AngularJS filter will work just fine in a web browser.

How to do it...

Here are the instructions to create a custom filter:

1. Create a new app using the *blank* template and go into the respective folder:

    ```
    $ ionic start Filter blank
    $ cd Filter
    ```

2. You need to install `angular-filter` so that you can use it in one of the examples:

    ```
    $ bower install angular-filter --save
    ```

3. Open the `index.html` file and include the dependency, as follows:

    ```
    <script src="lib/angular-filter/dist/
    angular-filter.js"></script>
    ```

4.   Then, replace the `<body>` tag with the following:

```html
<body ng-app="starter" ng-controller="MainCtrl">
  <ion-pane>
    <ion-header-bar class="bar-stable">
      <h1 class="title">Ionic Filter</h1>
    </ion-header-bar>
    <ion-content>
      <div class="list">
        <div class="item item-divider">
          Use $filter in controller
        </div>
        <label class="item item-input">
          <input type="text" placeholder="Type anything
          lowercase here" ng-model="data.lowercase">
        </label>
        <label class="item">
          {{ data.uppercase }}
        </label>
        <div class="item item-divider">
          Use angular-filter in interpolation
        </div>
        <label class="item">
          Max of [1,2,3,4,7,8,9] = {{ numberArray | max }}
        </label>
        <div class="item item-divider">
          Create custom filter
        </div>
        <label class="item" ng-repeat="item in
        countryCodes">
          {{ item }} <i class="icon ion-ios-arrow-
          thin-right"></i> {{ item | languageName }}
        </label>
      </div>
    </ion-content>
  </ion-pane>
</body>
```

The app will have three sections:

▸   How to tighten the input model in real time with a filter from the controller

▸   How to use the `angular-filter` module

▸   How to set up your own custom filter

5. Open `app.js` and edit it with the following code:

```
var app = angular.module('starter', ['ionic',
'angular.filter']);

app.controller('MainCtrl', function($scope, $filter) {
  $scope.data = {
    lowercase: '',
    uppercase: 'Resulted Upper Case'
  }

  $scope.$watch('data.lowercase', function(newVal,
  oldVal) {
    if (newVal != oldVal)
      $scope.data.uppercase = $filter('ucfirst')(newVal);
  });

  $scope.numberArray = [1,2,3,4,7,8,9];
  $scope.countryCodes = ["IN", "MX", "US", "GB", "FR"];
});
```

This code is used to set up your controller with some data so that it can be used in the filters.

6. Next, create a custom filter, as follows:

```
app.filter('languageName', function() {
  var codes = {
    "BR": "Brazil",
    "CA": "Canada",
    "CN": "China",
    "FR": "France",
    "DE": "Germany",
    "IN": "India",
    "IL": "Israel",
    "IT": "Italy",
    "MX": "Mexico",
    "US": "United States"
  }

  return function(input) {
    var output = codes[input] ? codes[input] : "Unknown";
    return output;
  }
});
```

This is a very simple, hardcoded example that demonstrates how to create a filter. The goal is to perform a conversion from the `input` value to the `output` value.

7. There is no need to customize any CSS. So, you can run and test the filter in the browser.

How it works...

You can use the AngularJS filter in the view or as a function in the controller or factory. It's considered a utility that simply converts or transforms any value to a desired value. There is no limitation on how you want to structure the filter.

In the first example of using `$filter` in the controller, you just use `$scope.$watch` on the input model and convert it in real time, as follows:

```
$scope.$watch('data.lowercase', function(newVal, oldVal) {
  if (newVal != oldVal)
    $scope.data.uppercase = $filter('ucfirst')(newVal);
});
```

You must declare `$filter` as a dependency for that controller.

The second example illustrates how a filter is used directly in the view without an interference of controller or factory:

```
{{ numberArray | max }}
```

AngularJS automatically detects the | sign and turns the value that is in front of it to an input. The `max` function will use it for conversion.

Finally, your last example is used to add the `languageName` filter. It's basically just a function that returns another function in the following format:

```
return function(input) {
  var output = codes[input] ? codes[input] : "Unknown";
  return output;
}
```

The value of the output will be what AngularJS renders in the view.

See also

▶   To understand more about the AngularJS filter, you can check out the official documentation at `https://docs.angularjs.org/api/ng/filter/filter`.

▶   `Angular-filter` has a wide range of filters to choose from. You can get a full list at `https://github.com/a8m/angular-filter`.

Animating an app using requestAnimationFrame with event binding

Animation is always a tricky part when it comes to mobile app development. The main reason behind this is that you really have to know how JavaScript or CSS animation works. Otherwise, if you use external libraries, you will run into performance problems such as jerky movements. In addition to this, there are many ways that can be used to bind an animation stage with a native touch event of the device. So, it always takes a little extra effort to get a good result.

In this recipe, you will learn how to:

 ▸ Detect a scroll event

 ▸ Bind the scroll position on pull down in order to slightly zoom the image

 ▸ The image zoom has exact ration is the scroll bounce

This example is similar to many apps with a profile page such as a Twitter iOS app. The top image can be the user's profile picture. The following is a screenshot of the app that you will build:

Getting ready

You can test this in a web browser. However, it's recommended that you use a physical device to test the animation performance, especially during fast scroll movements.

How to do it...

Here are the instructions to animate an app using `requestAnimationFrame` with event binding:

1. Create a new app using the *blank* template and go into the respective folder:

   ```
   $ ionic start ZoomOnScroll blank
   $ cd ZoomOnScroll
   ```

2. You need to set up the Sass dependencies, as follows:

   ```
   $ ionic setup sass
   ```

3. Open the `index.html` file and replace the `<body>` tag with the following:

   ```
   <body ng-app="starter" ng-controller="MyCtrl">

     <ion-header-bar class="bar-positive">
       <h1 class="title">My Photo Profile</h1>
     </ion-header-bar>

     <ion-content class="top-image" zoom-on-scroll>
       <ion-list>
         <ion-item ng-repeat="item in items">
           Item {{ item.id }}
         </ion-item>
       </ion-list>
     </ion-content>

   </body>
   ```

   There is no image element in this code, because the image is actually a part of the `<ion-content>` background.

4. Open `ionic.app.scss` placed under `scss` and add the following code:

   ```
   .top-image {
     padding-top: 150px!important;
   }

   .scroll-content {
     background-image: url('../img/sample.jpg');
     background-size: 100%;
     background-repeat: no-repeat;
   }
   ```

This will ensure that the content has 150 px of free space at the top, which will show the `sample.jpg` image.

5. Open `app.js` to edit with the following code:

```
var app = angular.module('starter', ['ionic']);

app.controller('MyCtrl', function($scope, $ionicScrollDelegate) {

  $scope.items = [];
  for (var i=1; i<=100; i++) {
    $scope.items.push({ id: i });
  }

});
```

6. To handle the animation interaction, you need to create the `zoomOnScroll` directive, which will be placed in `<ion-content>`:

```
app.directive('zoomOnScroll', function($ionicScrollDelegate) {
  return {
    link: function (scope, element, attrs) {
      ionic.DomUtil.ready(function() {

        var scrollContent =
        document.querySelector('.scroll-content'),
            windowHeight = $ionicScrollDelegate.
            _instances[0].element.clientHeight;
            windowWidth = $ionicScrollDelegate._
            instances[0].element.clientWidth;

        $ionicScrollDelegate.
        _instances[0].$element.bind('scroll', function(e) {

          function callback() {
            var scrollPosition = $ionicScrollDelegate.
            getScrollPosition().top,
                zoom = (-(scrollPosition*2 /
                windowHeight) + 1) * 100,
                offset = (windowWidth * ((zoom -
                100) / 100)) / 2;

            if (zoom > 100) {
              scrollContent.style['background-size']
              = zoom + '%';
              scrollContent.style['background-
              position-x'] = -offset + 'px';
```

```
            }
        }

        ionic.DomUtil.requestAnimationFrame(callback);

    });
});
}
};
});
```

 While you can use the regular method for animation or even a timeout event, in this case, it's better to use `ionic.DomUtil.requestAnimationFrame()` for improved performance. More on this will be discussed later.

7. Test run the app in the browser, as follows:

   ```
   $ ionic serve
   ```

8. Alternatively, you can perform a test run of the app in an iOS device when the phone is connected via a USB, as follows:

   ```
   $ ionic run –device
   ```

9. When you drag or pull down the list, the image will expand to zoom, as shown in the following screenshot (without distortion):

How it works...

Before explaining in depth, it's good to know about several limitations of this example. Some of these limitations are as follows:

▶ The code assumes that your top image is 150 px in height. This is just an arbitrary number and can be changed.

▶ The actual image size is 1280 x 853. So, if you want to swap out with other images, please consider testing the ratio properly (to avoid white space or missing corners).

▶ The image URL is fixed in the CSS. To have dynamic images (such as per user profile), you should populate the CSS `background-image` property properly from the AngularJS code.

▶ There is a potential performance impact for low-end Android devices. It's highly recommended that you build using Crosswalk for a better animation performance.

Let's start by taking a look at the `zoomOnScroll` directive. You should only start processing the DOM events when Ionic finishes its rendering:

```
ionic.DomUtil.ready()
```

Otherwise, you may get a *strange* bug when the binding sometimes happens and sometimes it does not.

There are some undocumented features of Ionic regarding `<ion-content>`. First, when you create a content area, it will insert a `div` element with the `scroll-content` class. That's why you should grab it in order to animate its background CSS properties, as follows:

```
var scrollContent = document.querySelector('.scroll-content')
```

Another area is the use of `$ionicScrollDelegate._instances[0].$element` to create a scroll binding. This scroll binding isn't available if you use a normal DOM element object.

To understand the scroll event and the data that you can get from it, you can output the variables from within the `callback()` function, as follows:

```
console.log(scrollPosition);
console.log(zoom);
console.log(offset);
```

What you will see is something like the following when the list content is pulled or dragged down:

```
-4.375
101.66349809885931
2.6615969581748917
-10
103.8022813688213
6.083650190114076
-27.5
110.45627376425855
16.730038022813687
-27.5
110.45627376425855
16.730038022813687
-43.75
116.63498098859316
26.61596958174905
-43.75
116.63498098859316
26.61596958174905
-48.75
118.5361216730038
29.657794676806088
```

The top position actually can be a negative number when it goes beyond the topmost position of the content area:

```
scrollPosition = $ionicScrollDelegate.getScrollPosition().top
```

That's where you take advantage of this feature to calculate the zoom ratio, which is the second line:

```
zoom = (-(scrollPosition*2 / windowHeight) + 1) * 100
```

The zoom value is just a percentage number to zoom the background image using the `background-size` CSS property. You can generate this ratio any way you like using the `scrollPosition` value. In this case, it is two times the amount of scrolling (to avoid seeing a white space area below the image).

However, this is not enough to complete this visual effect. You should also make sure that the zoomed image is at the center all the time. To do this, calculate the offset position, as follows:

```
offset = (windowWidth * ((zoom - 100) / 100)) / 2
```

This means that if the image is wider than the device's width, it should reposition the image to the left so that it stays in the middle.

Once all the required values are set, you just have to change the CSS properties of the `scrollContent` object, as follows:

```
scrollContent.style['background-size'] = zoom + '%';
scrollContent.style['background-position-x'] = -offset + 'px';
```

To improve the animation performance, you must use `requestAnimationFrame`, as follows:

```
ionic.DomUtil.requestAnimationFrame(callback);
```

 Ionic has abstracted the `requestAnimationFrame` function based on the native `window.requestAnimationFrame()` function. This feature works nicely with the browser rendering engine. In each second, the browser repaints the view approximately 60 times.

By calling `requestAnimationFrame`, you basically tell the browser to execute the `callback()` function before the next repaint. This is a great way to get into *alignment* with the rendering engine to make sure that you don't miss any frame. You may ask why people can't use the `setInterval()` method to manually inject the rendering code 60 times per second. It's simple to clarify that `setInterval()` does not obey the exact completion of the execution to ensure that it's executed 60 times per second.

There are always some short delays when you use `setInterval()`, and the 60 frames may run for over more than one second. For smooth animation, it's critical to understand this concept.

There's more...

The difference between the animation performances when using pure CSS transitions versus JavaScript has been an ongoing debate. However, with proper implementation of JavaScript, it has been tested and proven that JavaScript can make faster animation with a higher frame per second. An article, which can be viewed by visiting `http://davidwalsh.name/css-js-animation`, depicts some very useful facts.

Monitoring the frame rate in animation is extremely important. In general, the CSS transition is good for stateless and simple UI animation. JavaScript animation should be used when the animation is triggered by JavaScript and there is a granular transition process between state *A* and *B*. The example in this section is a good use of `requestAnimationFrame` because it's hard to predict the exact animation for the scrolling inputs from the device.

This example app is simple enough to help you just animate by changing the `background-size` and `background-position-x` properties. There are many high-performance animation engines in the market that can help you perform complex animation scenarios. You can check out Greensock (`http://www.greensock.com`) and Velocity.js (`http://velocityjs.org/`) to find out more.

8
User Registration and Authentication

In this chapter, we will cover the following tasks related to user management:

- Configuring a Facebook app with the Firebase authentication
- Configuring a Twitter app with the Firebase authentication
- Configuring a Google+ project with the Firebase authentication
- Creating an Ionic social authentication project for Facebook using `$firebaseAuth`
- Creating a LinkedIn app and configuring the authentication in Auth0
- Integrating Auth0's LinkedIn authentication in an Ionic project

Introduction

In this chapter, we will create three sample authentication apps:

▸ Social Authentication (Facebook, Twitter, and Google+) using Firebase

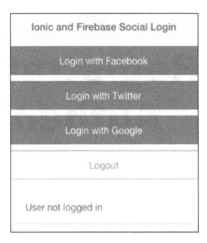

▸ Social Authentication (LinkedIn) using Auth0 and Firebase

Depending on the app, you may not need to use all of these authentication methods. For example, it would make more sense to use a LinkedIn authentication for an app focusing on a working professional to narrow down the audiences who fit the user profile of the app. Firebase supports many types of authentication with the exception of LinkedIn. Therefore, the LinkedIn authentication app will use a combination of Auth0 and Firebase.

The list of authentications supported in Firebase includes the following:

- Email and password
- Facebook
- Twitter
- GitHub
- Google
- Anonymous
- Custom

If you have your own authentication server where you maintain your own user database, you still can use the custom authentication of Firebase to create a custom token. You will see more details when you go through the LinkedIn authentication example, where Auth0 will ask Firebase for a custom token because Auth0 works with LinkedIn directly to authenticate users. You can use Auth0 for other authentication methods as well. It's really up to your app architecture. However, this chapter will try to simplify the authentication concept as much as possible. The sample apps will use Firebase as much as possible as a backend mechanism.

Configuring a Facebook app with Firebase authentication

Most of the time, your users already have a social media account somewhere. It's more convenient for them to log into your app using the same social account instead of filling out the same information again. Firebase provides an authentication feature to reduce the need to build a Facebook authentication module in AngularJS from scratch. As an app developer, you receive several benefits. The following are some of the advantages:

- An easier login option for users
- An increased registration conversion rate
- More information about users with their Facebook accounts
- Faster time to market as you don't have to build your own authentication mechanism

Getting ready

You need to have a Facebook account to log in and create a developer app. The account must be verified using a phone number or credit card number. You must make sure that there is a way to verify your account. A Google Voice phone number will not be allowed. Facebook will ask for account verification when you create the app. Hence, you don't have to do this up front.

How to do it...

In order for Firebase to authenticate users via the Facebook login, you have to create and configure the Facebook app to allow authentication and callback, as follows:

1. Log in to your Facebook account.

2. Navigate to `https://developers.facebook.com`.

3. Select **Add a New App** under the **My Apps** menu:

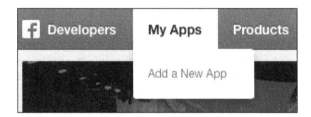

4. Select the **Website** button because we will be using JavaScript:

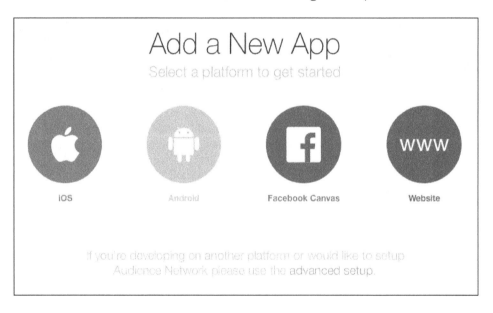

5. Provide the name of your app and click on the **Create New Facebook App ID** button. In this example, let's call it the `ionic_firebase_test` app:

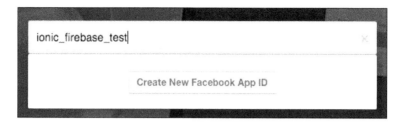

6. Choose any category that you want from the drop-down menu and click on **Create App ID**:

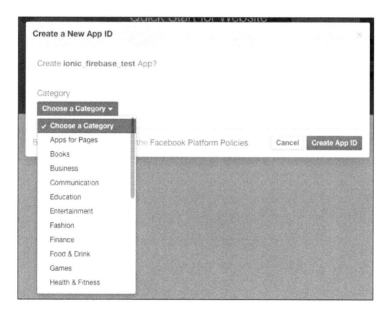

7. If you have not verified your Facebook account, at this step, Facebook will ask for verification. You can either add a phone number or credit card number to pass this step:

8. After the verification, go to the **Settings** menu in the left panel.

9. Click on the **Advanced** tab and change your *app restrictions or security* as needed for your app:

10. Under **OAuth Settings**, fill in the **Valid OAuth redirect URIs** input box with your own URL using the `https://auth.firebase.com/v2/<YOUR-FIREBASE>/auth/facebook/callback` format. So, if your Firebase app's name is `ionicebook`, it will look like what is shown in the following screenshot:

11. Scroll down to the end of the page and click on the **Save Changes** button.

This is the basic app configuration that you need to do for Facebook. Now, you will have to modify Firebase to enable the Facebook authentication, as follows:

12. While still in the same Facebook app screen, click on the **Basic** tab and select the **Show** button to reveal the App Secret string:

Basic	Advanced	Migrations
App ID	App Secret	
1579401235659574	2adc2ec2aa7e1fd7c122bb5f216347aa	Reset

13. Copy both the App ID and the App Secret string because you need to import them to Firebase.

14. Log in to your Firebase account and select your app (for example, `ionicebook`).

15. Click on the **Login & Auth** menu, which looks like this:

16. Click on the **Facebook** tab.

17. Provide the same Facebook App ID and App Secret string that you copied earlier:

18. Check off the **Enable Facebook Authentication** checkbox, and everything will be saved automatically.

How it works...

Firebase makes it very easy for you to work with the Facebook authentication because it takes care of server communication and builds in an API within AngularFire. You will explore the code in detail in the next section.

The authentication mechanism only needs the following three pieces of information:

- ▶ The Firebase Callback URL, so that Facebook knows how it should handle the redirect
- ▶ The Facebook App ID
- ▶ The Facebook Secret ID

You can trigger an authentication in the frontend simply by calling `$authWithOAuthPopup`.

There's more...

Firebase has a very good documentation on authentication that uses either an email and a password, or social accounts. Just visit `https://www.firebase.com/docs/web/guide/user-auth.html` for more information.

If you want to go ahead and dive into the code, Firebase also provides an interactive demo, which is hosted on `http://jsfiddle.net/firebase/a221m6pb/`.

Configuring a Twitter app with Firebase authentication

To authenticate using Twitter, Firebase also requires API Key and API Secret from your Twitter app. Firebase will take care of the communication and return the user object.

Getting ready

This is a straightforward process if you have already gone through the Facebook integration. It's similar to Twitter.

How to do it...

Here are the instructions to set up your Twitter app:

1. Log in to your Twitter account.
2. Navigate to `https://apps.twitter.com`.

3. Click on the **Create New App** button:

Provide the application details. You can fill in anything for description and website as Twitter will not check for a test app. Let's name the app as `ionic_firebase_test`. The most important field here is the **Callback URL**, as it must be in the `https://auth.firebase.com/v2/<YOUR-FIREBASE>/auth/twitter/callback` format. Since the Firebase app name is `ionicebook`, the callback URL will be `https://auth.firebase.com/v2/ionicebook/auth/twitter/callback`, as shown in the following screenshot:

Application Details

Name *

ionic_firebase_test

Your application name. This is used to attribute the source of a tweet and in user-facing authorization screens. 32 characters max.

Description *

Test Twitter Authentication for Ionic and Firebase

Your application description, which will be shown in user-facing authorization screens. Between 10 and 200 characters max.

Website *

http://www.PlaceholderIsOK.com

Your application's publicly accessible home page, where users can go to download, make use of, or find out more information about your application. This fully-qualified URL is used in the source attribution for tweets created by your application and will be shown in user-facing authorization screens.
(If you don't have a URL yet, just put a placeholder here but remember to change it later.)

Callback URL

https://auth.firebase.com/v2/ionicebook/auth/twitter/callback

Where should we return after successfully authenticating? OAuth 1.0a applications should explicitly specify their oauth_callback URL on the request token step, regardless of the value given here. To restrict your application from using callbacks, leave this field blank.

☑ Allow this application to be used to Sign in with Twitter

4. Check off the **Allow this application to be used to Sign in with Twitter** checkbox.

5. Check off the **Yes, I agree** checkbox for **Developer Agreement**:

Developer Agreement

New! We revised our Developer Agreement, effective as of May 18, 2015. Please read the updated Developer Agreement. By continuing to access or use our content or services after May 18, 2015, you agree to the revisions.

Last Update: October 22, 2014.

This Twitter Developer Agreement ("**Agreement**") is made between you (either an individual or an entity, referred to herein as "**you**") and Twitter, Inc., on behalf of itself and its worldwide affiliates (collectively, "**Twitter**") and governs your access to and use of the Licensed Material (as defined below).

PLEASE READ THE TERMS AND CONDITIONS OF THIS AGREEMENT CAREFULLY, INCLUDING WITHOUT LIMITATION ANY LINKED TERMS AND CONDITIONS APPEARING OR REFERENCED BELOW, WHICH ARE HEREBY MADE PART OF THIS LICENSE AGREEMENT. BY USING THE LICENSED MATERIAL, YOU ARE AGREEING THAT YOU HAVE READ, AND THAT YOU AGREE TO COMPLY WITH AND TO BE BOUND BY THE TERMS AND CONDITIONS OF THIS AGREEMENT AND ALL APPLICABLE LAWS AND REGULATIONS IN THEIR ENTIRETY WITHOUT LIMITATION OR QUALIFICATION. IF YOU DO NOT AGREE TO BE BOUND BY THIS AGREEMENT, THEN YOU MAY NOT ACCESS OR OTHERWISE USE THE LICENSED MATERIAL. THIS AGREEMENT IS EFFECTIVE AS OF THE FIRST DATE THAT YOU USE THE LICENSED MATERIAL ("**EFFECTIVE DATE**").

☐ Yes, I agree

Create your Twitter application

6. Click on the **Create your Twitter application** button.

7. Navigate to the **Keys and Access Tokens** tab:

ionic_firebase_test

Details   Settings   Keys and Access Tokens   Permissions

8. Under **Application Settings**, copy the API Key and API Secret:

Application Settings

Keep the "Consumer Secret" a secret. This key should never be human-readable in your application.

Consumer Key (API Key)   wHCVfUiHZpIzCyHnikrmL5mhH

Consumer Secret (API Secret)   MIIYKzoZdVmxlDBCBQ2hUftH90SIFe46ap73cfJxJg0U9bE6n7

You will need to provide Firebase the Twitter API Key and API Secret. Here are the steps:

9. Log in to your Firebase account and select your app (for example, `ionicebook`).

10. Click on the **Login & Auth** menu.

11. Click on the **Twitter** tab.

12. Provide the same Twitter API Key and API Secret that you copied earlier:

13. Check off the **Enable Twitter Authentication** checkbox, and everything will be saved automatically.

14. Don't close the **Firebase** tab or browser window, as you will be required to come back to provide information for the Google authentication later.

How it works...

The steps that we went through are used to set up the Twitter app correctly. If you already have an existing Twitter app, you can just use the API Key and API Secret from this app instead. As you have already seen, configuring on the side of Firebase to enable the Twitter authentication only takes two parameters. That's it.

Configuring a Google+ project with Firebase authentication

Google has a very comprehensive list of cloud services. Also, it's a good idea to include Google as your authentication mechanism due to a large number of users. In addition, Firebase is a Google company. Therefore, in the future, this process can be a lot simpler and you may have access to additional features.

Getting ready

If you don't already have a Google test account, you should create one.

How to do it...

Here are the instructions that are required to set up your Google+:

1. Navigate to `https://console.developers.google.com`.

2. Log in to your Google account.

3. Click on the **Create Project** button, as Google calls it a *project* rather than an *app*:

4. Fill in the name as `IonicFirebaseTest`, since Google does not allow the usage of a hyphen or an underscore:

5. Navigate to **APIs & auth** | **APIs** from the menu to the left:

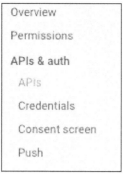

6. Under **OAuth**, click on the **Create new Client ID** button:

OAuth

OAuth 2.0 allows users to share specific
data with you (for example, contact lists)
while keeping their usernames, passwords,
and other information private.

Learn more

Create new Client ID

7. Provide the client ID details. Make sure that web application is checked, as we use JavaScript for the app. The **Authorized JavaScript origins** text box should have `https://auth.firebase.com`. The **Authorized redirect URIs** text box will have `https://auth.firebase.com/v2/ionicebook/auth/google/callback`, as the Firebase app name is `ionicebook`:

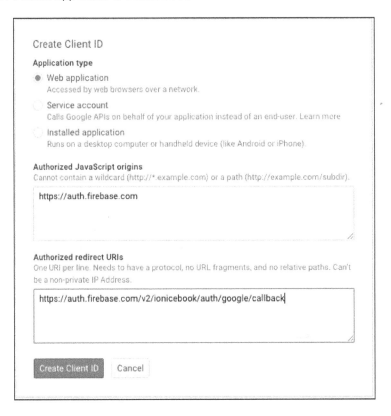

8. Click on the **Create Client ID** button to save the settings.

9. Under **Client ID for web application**, copy the client ID and client secret, which is used for Firebase:

Similarly, you will need to provide Firebase the Google client ID and client secret. The following are the steps that are required to accomplish this:

1. Log in to your Firebase account and select your app (for example, `ionicebook`).

2. Click on the **Login & Auth** menu.

3. Select the **Google** tab.

4. Provide the same Google client ID and client secret that you copied earlier:

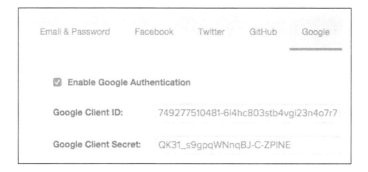

5. Check off the **Enable Google Authentication** checkbox, and everything will be saved automatically.

How it works...

There is no difference in terms of how Google, Facebook, and Twitter work for the OAuth authentication. However, note that the redirect or callback URLs for each method are a bit different. This is because Firebase has a different backend mechanism to handle each authentication endpoints.

Creating an Ionic social authentication project for Facebook using $firebaseAuth

So far, you have been just configuring the apps. This recipe will explain how easy it is to write the code to authenticate a user via Facebook, Twitter, or Google. You will go through an example app to set up a **login** button. The user will click on **login** to authenticate via his or her social network. Then, the app will display the basic profile information, including the user's picture. Finally, the user can click on **logout** to end the session.

Getting ready

The only thing that you need here is the Ionic CLI to perform the steps.

How to do it...

The following instructions are used to code for the Facebook authentication:

1. Create a blank Ionic app (for example, `SocialAuth`), as follows:

   ```
   $ ionic start SocialAuth blank
   ```

2. Go to the project folder:

   ```
   $ cd SocialAuth
   ```

3. For authentication to work on a physical device, it will need two Cordova plugins, `InAppBrowser` and `Cookies`. The reason is that the authentication popup window will show in another browser window. Also, for Firebase to work, it needs native cookie support in the app. Type the following two command lines in your app folder:

   ```
   $ cordova plugin add org.apache.cordova.inappbrowser


   $ cordova plugin add https://github.com/bez4pieci/Phonegap-
   Cookies-Plugin.git
   ```

4. Open the `index.html` file under `/www` to edit the main template.

5. Install the Firebase and AngularFire modules:

   ```
   $ sudo bower install angularfire –save --allow-root
   ```

6. Add the Firebase and AngularFire modules:

   ```
   <!-- Firebase -->
   <script src="lib/firebase/firebase.js"></script>


   <!-- AngularFire -->
   <script src="lib/angularfire/dist/angularfire.js"></script>
   ```

7. Under `<body ng-app="starter">`, replace with the following code because you will show four buttons—**Facebook**, **Twitter**, **Google**, and **Logout**. Then, after logging in, the UI will display some basic user profile in the user object:

   ```
   <ion-pane>
     <ion-header-bar class="bar-stable">
   ```

```html
      <h1 class="title">Ionic and Firebase Social Login</h1>
    </ion-header-bar>

    <ion-content ng-controller="LoginCtrl">
      <!-- Buttons -->
      <button class="button button-full button-positive"
      ng-click="login(providerConf[0])">Login with
      Facebook</button>
      <button class="button button-full button-positive"
      ng-click="login(providerConf[1])">Login with
      Twitter</button>
      <button class="button button-full button-positive"
      ng-click="login(providerConf[2])">Login with
      Google</button>
      <button class="button button-full button-outline
      button-assertive" ng-click="logout()">Logout</button>

      <!-- Logged-in user text -->
      <div class="card" ng-hide="user">
        <div class="item item-text-wrap">User not
        logged in</div>
        <!-- <div class="item item-text-wrap"
        ng-bind="user.uid"></div> -->
      </div>
      <div class="list" ng-show="user">
        <a class="item item-thumbnail-left" href="#">
          <img ng-src="{{ user.avatar }}">
          <h2>{{ user.name }}</h2>
          <p>{{ user.uid }}</p>
          <p>{{ user.email }}</p>
        </a>
      </div>
    </ion-content>
  </ion-pane>
```

8. Open `app.js` under `/www/js` to edit it.

9. Make sure that you include `firebase` in the module:

   ```js
   var app = angular.module("starter", ["ionic", "firebase"]);
   ```

10. Keep `app.run()` the same, as that will not change for this project. However, delete all the other boilerplate if it exists. You will create the Auth factory and the `LoginCtrl` controller.

11. Add the Auth factory as follows because you will need to call `login()` and
`logout()` and get the user profile data via `onAuth()`. Calling `Firebase()` with
your Firebase URL will create a reference object for you to work with:

```
// create a custom Auth factory to handle $firebaseAuth
app.factory('Auth', function($firebaseAuth, $timeout){
  var ref = new
  Firebase('https://ionicebook.firebaseio.com');
  var auth = $firebaseAuth(ref);

  return {
    // helper method to login with multiple providers
    login: function (provider, options) {
      var result;
      if (options)
        result = auth.$authWithOAuthPopup(
        provider, {scope: options});
      else
        result = auth.$authWithOAuthPopup(provider);
      return result;
    },
    // wrapping the unauth function
    logout: function () {
      auth.$unauth();
    },
    // wrap the $onAuth function with $timeout so it
    processes
    // in the digest loop.
    onAuth: function (callback) {
      auth.$onAuth(function(authData) {
        $timeout(function() {
          callback(authData);
        });
      });
    }
  };
});
```

12. Create the `LoginCtrl` controller with some initial values in `$scope`, as follows:

```
app.controller("LoginCtrl", function($scope, Auth) {
  // Initially set no user to be logged in
  $scope.user = null;
```

```
    // Assign permission request per provider
    $scope.providerConf = [
      {
        name: "facebook",
        options: "email,user_likes,
        publish_actions,user_about_me,read_stream"
      },
      {
        name: "twitter"
        // Twitter has no permission object so
        we don't have to pass the options string
      },
      {
        name: "google",
        options: "profile,email,openid"
      },
    ];
  });
```

13. Within the `LoginCtrl` controller, add the `login()` function to `$scope` so that the frontend can access it. This is done so that the three login buttons just pass the proper provider string to trigger the login via Firebase:

```
// Calls $authWithOAuthPopup on $firebaseAuth
// This will be processed by the InAppBrowser
   plugin on mobile
// We can add the user to $scope here or in the $onAuth fn
$scope.login = function scopeLogin(providerObj) {

  Auth.login(providerObj.name, providerObj.options)
  .then(function(authData){
    console.log('We are logged in ' +
    providerObj.name + ' !', authData);
  })
  .catch(function(error) {
    console.error(error);
  });
};
```

14. Assign the `logout()` function straight from the factory. This is also for the `logout` button to call:

```
// Logs a user out
$scope.logout = Auth.logout;
```

15. Finally, you need to customize the user object based on whether it's a Facebook, Twitter, or Google login. The main reason behind this is that each method returns its own social network profile object. You want a uniform way in order to render the user profile correctly in the template:

```
// detect changes in authentication state
// when a user logs in, set them to $scope
Auth.onAuth(function(authData) {
  $scope.user = authData;
  console.log(authData);
  if ($scope.user) {
    switch ($scope.user.provider) {
      case "facebook":
        $scope.user.avatar = authData.facebook
        .cachedUserProfile.picture.data.url;
        $scope.user.name = authData.facebook.displayName;
        $scope.user.email = authData.facebook.email;
        break;
      case "twitter":
        $scope.user.avatar = authData.twitter
        .cachedUserProfile.profile_image_url;
        $scope.user.name = authData.twitter.displayName;
        $scope.user.email = authData.twitter
        .cachedUserProfile.description;
        break;
      case "google":
        $scope.user.avatar = authData
        .google.cachedUserProfile.picture;
        $scope.user.name = authData.google.displayName;
        $scope.user.email = authData.google.email;
        break;
    }
  }
});
```

16. Go back to the console and test in your browser. Make sure that you run the following command line in your project folder and not the /www folder:

```
$ ionic serve
```

17. You should be able to see the login screen, as shown in the following screenshot:

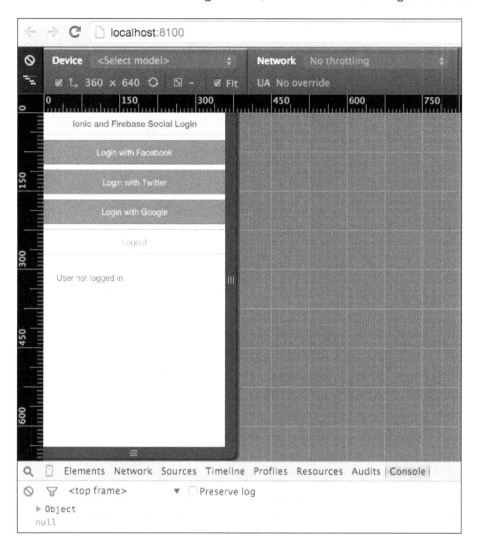

18. When you click on the **Facebook** button and log in, you should be able to see your avatar, name, and email:

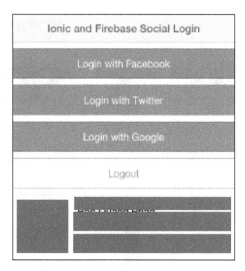

19. Take a look at the console and see more details of the user object. You can expand on the app and use any data that you like.

Note that for production deployment, you may want to remove all the `console.log()` outputs because it's not a good idea to reveal information to the end users (if they decided to turn on the debug functionality in a browser):

How it works...

The key for the social login to work is calling `$authWithOAuthPopup`. You can pass a provider string (such as `"facebook"`, `"twitter"`, and `"google"`) for this and indicate which social network you want to use. Firebase will take care of the entire login process and return the user's profile data in an `authData` object. You can do anything you want with this object.

In the preceding example, the code will take some important fields (`email`, `avatar`, `ID`, and `name`) and assign them to the `$scope.user` object. This is how Angular detects and updates the template on the frontend. Each social network has its own object structure. That's why you have to detect it via switch (`$scope.user.provider`) { } (or if-else) and properly get the value from the `authData` object.

There's more...

For testing and development, you can request for any permission. However, if you want to publish the Facebook app in production, you need to go through a review process. This may take a few days. For more information on this, visit `https://developers.facebook.com/docs/facebook-login/permissions/v2.5`, the Facebook developer website.

Creating a LinkedIn app and configuring authentication in Auth0

Firebase does not support LinkedIn natively, but it does allow the creation of a custom token. This method is used mainly when the authentication mechanism is actually performed somewhere else, either on your own server or another SaaS provider. In this case, you will be using Auth0 to provide the LinkedIn authentication. You could have performed the Facebook, Twitter, or Google authentication via Auth0 as well. However, it's recommended to use Firebase as much as possible as it's simpler to use. This is not only due to cost-related reasons, but also for the reduction of the number of integration points and code complexity.

Getting ready

Account registration is required for Auth0, Firebase, and LinkedIn in order to perform the steps in this recipe.

How to do it...

You need to configure your app in Auth0 first by performing the following steps:

1. Sign up for an Auth0 account and navigate to `https://manage.auth0.com/`.
2. You will see the dashboard first, but there is nothing there yet because there is no app defined. To create an app, click on the **New App/API** button:

3. Give the app a name, as follows:

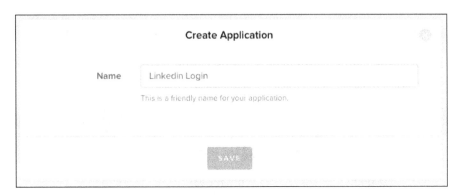

4. You can ignore the first **Quick Start** tab because it's better to learn through specific details inside the app. Select the **Setting** tab and fill out the form. Let's assume that we used `ionicebook` as the domain name when creating the account. The callback URL will be `https://ionicebook.auth0.com/mobile` and **Allowed Origins (CORS)** will have the value `file://*, http://localhost:8100/`. The reason behind this is that you have to tell Auth0 that it is OK to get the REST calls from these URLs. If you run the app in your physical device, it will call from a file system (`file://`). If you run the URL via a browser from a local server (`ionic serve`), it will be `http://localhost:8100/`:

5. Navigate to the **Addons** tab:

6. Select the Firebase icon:

7. A dialog will appear for you to provide the Firebase Secret. If you don't have that ready, go to the Firebase app and navigate to the **Secrets** tab:

8. Click on the **Show** button below the input box and then copy the whole secret string, as shown in the following screenshot:

9. Go back to the Auth0 app and paste to the LinkedIn add-on:

4. Copy the **Secret** and paste it here:

Firebase Secret | o4LrKyVDGf8STb8ll7CJV9J9CbTcliS3T2lS6· | SAVE

Get the secret from your Firebase dashboard.

10. Click on **Save**.

That's it as regards to configuring Auth0 and Firebase. However, you still need to connect to LinkedIn. Before changing anything in Auth0, you must get the LinkedIn API and Secret Key to provide to Auth0. The following are the steps that are required to set up a LinkedIn app:

1. Create a LinkedIn account if you don't already have one and log in.

2. Navigate to `https://www.linkedin.com/developer/apps`.

3. Click on the **Create Application** button:

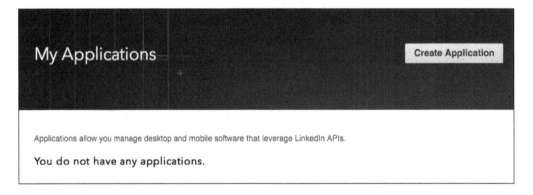

My Applications   Create Application

Applications allow you manage desktop and mobile software that leverage LinkedIn APIs.

You do not have any applications.

4. Fill out the form as shown in the following screenshot. The most important part is that you need to have Website URL as either `http://localhost:8100`, or whatever URL you will be using to test the app. You can change this later once it's in production:

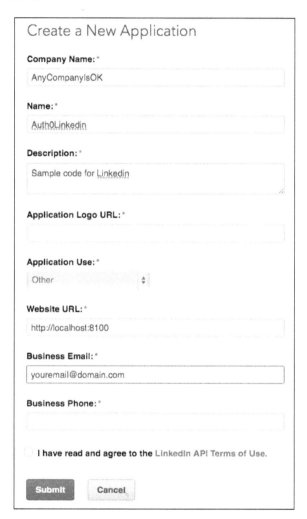

5. Make sure that you check off **Terms of Use** and click on the **Submit** button.

6. Navigate to the **Authentication** menu to the left. It should be available on the first page.

7. Copy the client ID and client Secret. You will use those for the Auth0 inputs:

8. Make sure that you check off the permission that you want to acquire from the users. In this example, let's check off all the checkboxes so that you can see what LinkedIn returns in the authentication:

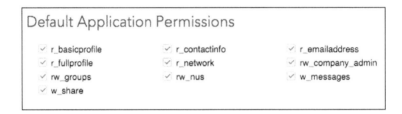

9. In order for the authentication process to know the callback, you need to provide that information in the OAuth inputs. It will be your Auth0 URL, with the trailing `/login/callback` instance in the URL:

10. Navigate to the **Settings** tab from the menu to the left and ensure that
    Application Status is **Development**. You will need to switch this to **Live** when
    you go into production:

11. Navigate to the **JavaScript** tab and make sure that **Valid SDK Domains** is
    `http://localhost:8100/` or whatever local URL for development:

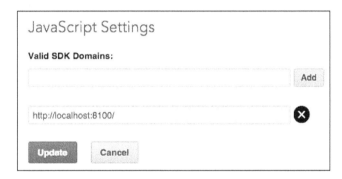

12. Click on the **Update** button to finish configuring your LinkedIn app.

At this point, you have completed setting up Auth0, connecting it to Firebase and creating your own LinkedIn app. However, there is one more thing that is required to complete the process, and that thing is the connection of the Auth0 and LinkedIn app. Otherwise, Auth0 will not know where to send the data to. This can be done in a few simple steps:

1. Navigate to the Auth0 app and browse to **Connections | Social** from the menu to the left:

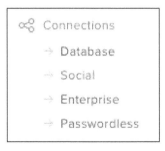

2. Click on the **Linkedin** icon:

3. Fill in the API Key and Secret Key that you copied earlier from the LinkedIn app. Make sure that you check off the attributes and permissions that you want. In this example, you can check off all of them to review the kind of data that will be returned from LinkedIn:

4. Navigate to the **Apps** tab in the menu at the top:

5. Make sure that your Auth0 app (such as **Linkedin Login**) is checked off with the green toggle button.

6. Click on **Save**.

How it works...

So far, you have not written a single line of code. This is because Auth0 and Firebase will take care of the backend data exchange so that the user will be authenticated via LinkedIn. In the next section, you will take a look at how simple it is to actually authenticate a user and get the returned user object.

The way it works in this setup is as follows:

1. Auth0 acts as a trigger to call the LinkedIn API to exchange user data.

2. Once LinkedIn says, **"Okay, this user is authenticated"**, Firebase will get the object and store it in the memory. At the same time, Auth0 will ask Firebase to create a custom token to pass data to Firebase.

3. Firebase will then agree to authenticate on its own backend and allow the user to get data from the Firebase database.

4. Ionic will act as the frontend entirely and only render the data, as returned from the APIs. You will explore more possibilities in this area later on.

There's more...

Auth0 made it easy by providing you with a wizard depending on how you build the app (for instance, by using an add-on or a third-party plugin). You can download the *seed project* from Auth0. However, you need to be aware that the app tends to have more boilerplate than the most basic code, which will be discussed in the next recipe. The seed project has a full-blown navigation with routes and templates. You will explore more about those topics in other chapters.

In case you want to use the seed project, the following are the steps:

1. Go to your app page and under the **Quick Start** tab, let's select **Hybrid Mobile App** because Auth0 has specific steps defined for Ionic and Firebase already:

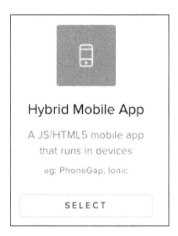

2. Next, select **Ionic** in the SDK list:

3. Select **Firebase** under **3rd Party API**:

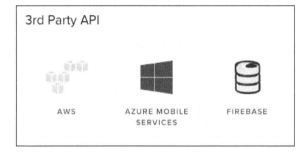

4. Click on the **Download A Seed Project** button:

It will be useful to know where the Auth0 app is being authorized within the test user LinkedIn account. During testing and development, you may have to manually remove this authorization once in awhile. The reason behind this is that there may be some cache or bugs. Removing the authentication in the test user will let you start from scratch.

The following is the process that provides the details of how to do this:

1. Log in as a LinkedIn test user (not the LinkedIn account that has the app, even though it can be the same).

2. In the top-right menu, navigate to **Privacy & Settings**:

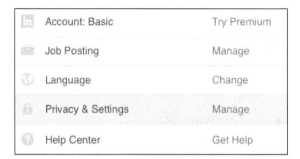

3. Navigate to **Groups, Companies & Applications** from the menu to the left:

4. Click on the **View your applications** link:

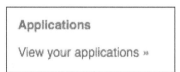

5. If you have been testing the app, you will see the app name in the list. All you need to do is to check off the app name and click on **Remove**:

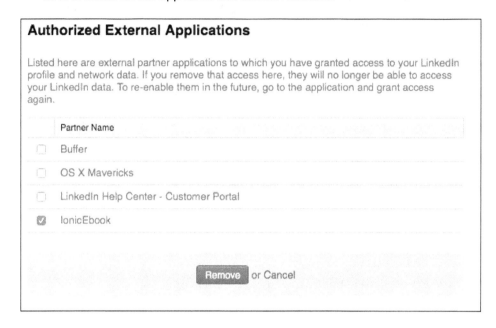

6. After removing the app, the clean list should not have your Auth0 app name any more. Your list could look different from the one shown in the following screenshot, depending on the other apps that you have authorized in the past:

Authorized External Applications

Listed here are external partner applications to which you have granted access to your LinkedIn profile and network data. If you remove that access here, they will no longer be able to access your LinkedIn data. To re-enable them in the future, go to the application and grant access again.

	Partner Name
☐	Buffer
☐	OS X Mavericks
☐	LinkedIn Help Center - Customer Portal

Remove or Cancel

Integrating Auth0's LinkedIn authentication in an Ionic project

Once you have set up Auth0, Firebase, and LinkedIn, the boilerplate code that is needed to authenticate a user is very simple. This is the beauty of using Auth0 for this process. In this recipe, you will learn how to go through an app development that is similar to that of the app that you created earlier for Twitter, Facebook, and Google. Basically, a user will click on **Login** to make an authentication dialog pop up. After being authenticated, the app will show the profile photo, name, unique ID, and email address.

Getting ready

You can start from scratch by creating a blank Ionic app. It's faster to make a copy of the previous Firebase app and change a few lines of code.

How to do it...

You only need to write code in two files, `index.html` and `app.js`:

1. You need to download the required modules from Auth0. All of them are located in Auth0's `auth0-ionic` example. Navigate to `https://github.com/auth0/auth0-ionic/tree/master/examples/firebase-sample/www/lib` and download `auth0-lock`, `auth0-angular`, `angular-jwt`, `firebase`, and `angularfire`.

2. Include these modules in `index.html`. It will look like this:

   ```html
   <script src="lib/auth0-lock/build/
   auth0-lock.js"></script>
   <!-- ionic/angularjs js -->
   <script src="lib/ionic/js/ionic.bundle.js"></script>

   <script src="lib/auth0-angular/build/
   auth0-angular.js"></script>
   <script src="lib/angular-jwt/dist/
   angular-jwt.js"></script>
   <script src="lib/firebase/firebase.js"></script>
   <script src="lib/angularfire/dist/
   angularfire.js"></script>
   ```

3. Just like in the social authentication app using Firebase, you will need a **Login** and **Logout** button and a place to display some basic user profile. Just change the HTML under the `<body>` tag to the following:

```html
<ion-pane>
  <ion-header-bar class="bar-stable">
    <h1 class="title">Linkedin Authentication</h1>
  </ion-header-bar>

  <ion-content ng-controller="LoginCtrl">
    <!-- Buttons -->
    <button class="button button-full button-positive"
    ng-click="login()">Login with Linkedin</button>
    <button class="button button-full button-outline
    button-assertive" ng-click="logout()">Logout</button>

    <!-- Logged-in profile text -->
    <div class="card" ng-hide="profile">
      <div class="item item-text-wrap">User not
      logged in</div>
    </div>
    <div class="list" ng-show="profile">
      <a class="item item-thumbnail-left" href="#">
        <img ng-src="{{ profile.picture }}">
        <h2>{{ profile.name }}</h2>
        <p>{{ profile.user_id }}</p>
        <p>{{ profile.email }}</p>
      </a>
    </div>
  </ion-content>
</ion-pane>
```

4. Open and edit `/www/js/app.js`.

5. You need a global variable to keep track of the session data. This is just for simplicity, as the best practice is to keep this in local storage or a cookie within `$scope`. More information on this will be discussed later.

```js
var LINKEDIN = {};
```

6. Your app must include the modules that we downloaded earlier:

```
var app = angular.module('starter', [
  'ionic',
  'auth0',
  'angular-jwt',
  'firebase'
]);
```

7. There is no change within `app.run()`. So, let's leave it as is.

8. Unlike Firebase login, Auth0 requires some configuration in your AngularJS app. First, it initializes `authProvider` with your Auth0 information. Note that the `clientID` variable is the same client ID string from your Auth0 app. Then, you need to tell Auth0 to send the authentication token string each time an API is called to Firebase. That's why you set up the function in `jwtInterceptorProvider` and push it to `$httpProvider`:

```
app.config(function(authProvider, jwtInterceptorProvider,
$httpProvider) {
  // Configure Auth0
  authProvider.init({
    domain: 'ionicebook.auth0.com',
    clientID: 'eVuc9hYlogywlBFmSA89QuO2bif6oC3J',
    loginState: 'login'
  });

  jwtInterceptorProvider.tokenGetter = function(store,
  jwtHelper, auth) {
    var idToken = LINKEDIN.token;
    var refreshToken = LINKEDIN.refreshToken;
    if (!idToken || !refreshToken) {
      return null;
    }
    if (jwtHelper.isTokenExpired(idToken)) {
      return auth.refreshIdToken(refreshToken).
      then(function(idToken) {
        LINKEDIN.token = idToken;
        return idToken;
      });
    } else {
      return idToken;
    }
  }
}
```

```
    $httpProvider.interceptors.push('jwtInterceptor');
});
```

9. You need to write the code for the `LoginCtrl` controller. This will have two functions: `login()` and `logout()`, as follows:

```
app.controller('LoginCtrl', function($scope, $rootScope,
auth) {
  $scope.login = function() {
    auth.signin({
      closable: false,
      // This asks for the refresh token
      // So that the user never has to log in again
      authParams: {
        scope: 'openid offline_access'
      }
    }, function(profile, idToken, accessToken, state,
    refreshToken) {
      LINKEDIN.profile = profile;
      $scope.profile = profile;
      console.log('profile:');
      console.log(profile);
      LINKEDIN.token = idToken;
      LINKEDIN.refreshToken = refreshToken;
      auth.getToken({
        api: 'firebase'
      }).then(function(delegation) {
        console.log('delegation:');
        console.log(delegation);
      }, function(error) {
        console.log("There was an error logging in",
        error);
      })
    }, function(error) {
      console.log("There was an error logging in", error);
    });
  }

  $scope.logout = function() {
    auth.signout();
    LINKEDIN = {};
    $scope.profile = undefined;
  }
});
```

10. There are many lines with `console.log()`. The goal is to output the entire object so that you can inspect its data. After saving both the files, you can test these on the browser, as follows:

```
$ ionic serve
```

11. Authenticate via the LinkedIn test user's account and open the browser console. You should be able to inspect the profile object and the delegation object that is passed to Firebase:

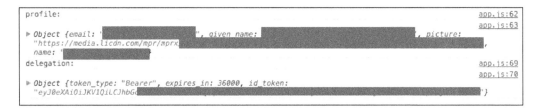

How it works...

Note that the login modal is not from the current code. It was a ready-to-use template from Auth0 when you included `auth0-lock.js`. You don't have to use this template, but it's convenient for the purpose of this recipe. The `signin()` function does the majority of the work to authenticate the user and return the profile object. Then, you will need to use the `getToken()` function to encapsulate the data in a JSON object so that it can be given to Firebase. Later, we will also define how Firebase uses this information to create a custom token using `authWithCustomToken()` as well. The basic mechanism is that Firebase will receive all the profile data and use the information to properly decide upon the user permission using the security rule of Firebase. For example, your app only allows authenticated users to have access to their own data. Therefore, you need to map the email address to `userId` and ensure that `userId` is the same as `ownerId`.

See also

This recipe does not cover local storage, because when the app is closed and the user comes back, they can still be authenticated automatically without having to log in to LinkedIn again. You will learn more about local storage using JavaScript and Cordova plugin in the later chapters of this book.

9
Saving and Loading Data Using Firebase

In this chapter, we will cover the following tasks related to persistent data operations using Firebase:

- ▸ Saving array data to Firebase
- ▸ Rendering a large Firebase data set using collection-repeat
- ▸ Saving form data to Firebase

Introduction

You will learn how to send and receive data between Ionic and a backend server, which is Firebase in our case. As an app developer, you will want to spend more time on building a solution for your customers than building a backend server with a database on your own. Firebase can act as a real-time database so that your app data can be synchronized between the database, frontend model objects, and the view layer (that is, what users actually see). This three-way binding is powerful because it simplifies many complex implementation scenarios such as the following:

- ▸ Chatting or messaging when there are multiple users sending and receiving data
- ▸ Saving a multistep form's data
- ▸ A real-time collaboration app that requires you to save a complex dataset
- ▸ A real-time data feed for a social networking app

The key benefits of Firebase as a backend database is that you can ensure that there is a very low latency between saving data to the server and receiving an acknowledgement. This is very critical in mobile app development, where the response time is critical to ensure a good user experience.

All the examples in this chapter will use AngularFire because it already has all the API operations provided for objects and arrays such as `add`, `remove`, `save`, and `get`. More information about the AngularFire API can be found at `https://www.firebase.com/docs/web/libraries/angular/api.html`.

If you have used AngularFire before the release of version 1.0, there have been some changes in the API implementation. Firebase has made the migration guide available at `https://www.firebase.com/docs/web/libraries/angular/migration-guides.html`.

Saving array data to Firebase

Sending and saving data to the Firebase backend server is as simple as calling the `$add()` function. Firebase automatically handles all the REST operations so that you don't have to call via the `$http` services or create your own. From a frontend developer's perspective, you can treat your data as a typical JavaScript object.

In this recipe, you will learn how to make connections to Firebase by creating a reference object and adding data into the object in the array format. Firebase treats an array like an object. The only difference is that each array's item will have an integer key. Here's an example:

```
// When we send this
['a', 'b', 'c', 'd', 'e']
// Firebase stores this
{0: 'a', 1: 'b', 2: 'c', 3: 'd', 4: 'e'}
```

Getting ready

You should log in to your Firebase dashboard ahead of time and navigate to the **Data** tab. The code will create a node called `items` to store data. You need to make sure that there is no existing `items` node, in case you created one before.

How to do it...

Here are the instructions for adding 100 items in the `items` array stored in Firebase:

1. Create a blank Ionic app (such as `firebase-ionic`) and change the directory to that folder:

   ```
   $ ionic start firebase-ionic blank
   ```

2. Edit `index.html` to make sure that Firebase and AngularFire (below `ionic.bundle.js`) are included:

   ```
   <script src="lib/firebase/firebase-v2.2.4.js"></script>
   <script src="lib/firebase/
   angularfire-v1.1.1.min.js"></script>
   ```

You may wish to confirm with Firebase documentation for the latest versions and compatibility between Firebase and AngularFire. This example uses Firebase v2.2.4 and AngularFire v1.1.1 because they were the latest releases.

4. Open `app.js` to edit it. You may want to delete its entire contents because you will rewrite most of it.

5. Create two variables: `app` for the starter app and `ref` for the Firebase reference:

```
var app = angular.module('starter', ['ionic', 'firebase']);
var ref = new
Firebase('https://ionicbook.firebaseio.com/items/');
```

The `items` node does not need to exist in your Firebase application prior to creating a JavaScript reference to it. Firebase will automatically create it in the backend. If you want to create any node to store data, all you need to do is append the name in the URL. You should replace `ionicbook` with your own Firebase account.

6. Create the `app.run()` function as follows:

```
app.run(function($ionicPlatform, $firebaseArray,
$timeout) {
  $ionicPlatform.ready(function() {
    // Hide the accessory bar by default (remove this
    to show the accessory bar above the keyboard
    // for form inputs)
    if(window.cordova && window.cordova.plugins.Keyboard) {
      cordova.plugins.Keyboard.
      hideKeyboardAccessoryBar(true);
    }
    if(window.StatusBar) {
      StatusBar.styleDefault();
    }

  });

  // $firebaseArray is new in 1.0.0
  // Instructions to migrate from previous version:
  // https://www.firebase.com/docs/web/
    libraries/angular/migration-guides.html
  var items = $firebaseArray(ref);

  // Wait for items array to load from server
  items.$loaded().then(function(data) {
```

```
      console.log('Number of items = ' + data.length);

      // If there is no data, then add 100 items to the array
      if (data.length == 0) {
        for (var i=0; i<100; i++) {
          data.$add({
            name: "Item " + i,
            $priority: i // Priority is used to ensure
            they are displayed in order
          });
        }
      }
    })
  });
```

7. Go to the command line and run the app using `ionic serve`.

8. Navigate back to the **Data** tab of Firebase.

9. You should be able to see 100 records inserted in the `items` node, as shown in the following screenshot:

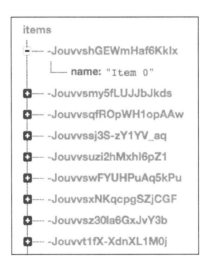

How it works...

So far, you have not done anything in the Ionic interface. The preceding code only inserts 100 records in the `items` node in Firebase. This operation must happen within `items.$loaded().then()` because you have to ensure that Firebase finished its initialization of the connection. Then, for each record, you loop through a simple for loop and call `$add()`. The code also adds `$priority` in the JSON object. This is optional, because you want the data to be displayed properly in order later on. You can have any key and value in this JSON object.

Rendering a large Firebase data set using collection-repeat

When your app grows, the size of the database also grows. Typically, there are many ways to handle large datasets such as paging, caching, and filtering. However, there is a very useful feature in Ionic that allows you to repeat through a large list of items without sacrificing performance. Ionic's `collection-repeat` is similar to AngularJs' `ng-repeat`. The main difference is its rendering mechanism. Most of the time, the app does not need to render thousands of items at once. So, `collection-repeat` accesses only a subset of the data and binds it to the current page, where it is visible to the user.

Getting ready

You will continue to work on the previous app. There are some modifications in `index.html` and `app.js`.

How to do it...

Here is how you can retrieve data and add, edit, and delete items:

1. Open `index.html` to edit it.

2. Insert the following code within `<body>`:

```
<ion-pane ng-controller="ItemCtrl">
  <ion-header-bar class="bar-calm item-input-inset">
    <label class="item-input-wrapper">
      <i class="icon ion-plus placeholder-icon"></i>
      <input type="text" placeholder="Insert New Item"
      ng-model="newItem">
    </label>
    <button class="button button-positive"
    ng-click="add(newItem); newItem='';">
      Add
    </button>
  </ion-header-bar>
  <ion-content>
    <ion-list>
      <ion-item class="item item-avatar"
      collection-repeat="item in items">
        <img src="http://placehold.it/40x40">
        <h2>{{ item.name }}</h2>
        <p>Description for {{ item.name }}</p>
```

```
          <ion-option-button class="button-dark"
          ng-click="edit(item)">
            Edit
          </ion-option-button>
          <ion-option-button class="button-assertive"
          ng-click="delete(item)">
            Delete
          </ion-option-button>
        </ion-item>
      </ion-list>
    </ion-content>
  </ion-pane>
```

You will write some code in app.js to handle ItemCtrl later. The preceding code is very simple, as it will perform the following functions:

- ❑ It can render all the items in a list.

- ❑ If you swipe left, it shows the **Edit** and **Delete** buttons. This can be done via `<ion-option-button>`. You should always use it within the `<ion-list>` and `<ion-item>` hierarchy because that is how Ionic structures the directives.

- ❑ The top header bar will have an input box and an **Add** button to add new records.

3. When a user edits an entry, there will be a modal popup with an input box to change the value of that entry. You need a template for the content of this Ionic modal. So, insert the following code after `<ion-pane>`:

```
<script type="text/ng-template" id="edit.html">
  <ion-modal-view>
    <ion-header-bar>
      <h1 class="title">Edit Item</h1>
    </ion-header-bar>
    <ion-content>
      <div class="list">
        <label class="item item-input">
          <span class="input-label">Name</span>
          <input type="text" ng-model="editedItem.name">
        </label>
      </div>
      <button class="button button-full
      button-positive" ng-click="save()">
        Save
      </button>
      <button class="button button-full
      button-stable" ng-click="close()">
```

```
        Cancel
      </button>
    </ion-content>
  </ion-modal-view>
</script>
```

You can place the template code anywhere, either inside a `<script>` tag or in a separate HTML file, which needs to be linked either via a router or an Ionic modal delegate. This modal has *wired* the `editedItem.name` model to the input box. When a user clicks on the **Save** button, it will call the `save()` function to send data to Firebase.

4. Now, let's work on `app.js` to create the logic in your `ItemCtrl`:

```
app.controller('ItemCtrl', function($scope,
$firebaseArray, $ionicModal, $ionicListDelegate) {

  $scope.items = $firebaseArray(ref);
  $scope.editedItem = {};

  $scope.items.$loaded().then(function(data) {
    // Start the priority value which is lower
      than previous
    // The lower the value, the higher it is
      appearing on the list
    $scope.newPriority = (data.length > 0)
    ? data[0].$priority - 1 : -1;
    console.log("Items have been loaded:");
    console.log(data);
  });

  // Load template for modal to edit an item
  $ionicModal.fromTemplateUrl('edit.html', {
    scope: $scope,
    animation: 'slide-in-up'
  }).then(function(modal) {
    $scope.modal = modal;
  });
});
```

You need to load the Firebase data again to `$scope.items` so that the view has access to the array. After the data is loaded, `$scope.newPriority` is assigned with a value that is smaller than the latest priority value in the zero index of the array. The `$ionicModal.fromTemplateUrl()` function is also called to load the template in the memory. Then, the entire modal directive is assigned to the `$scope.modal` object. This will allow you to programmatically show and hide the modal later.

5. Also, within `ItemCtrl`, you need to add those functions to handle interactions from the view layer:

```
$scope.add = function(val) {
  if (!val || val.length === 0 || !val.trim()) {
    alert("Your value is invalid");
  } else {
    $scope.items.$add({
      name: val,
      $priority: $scope.newPriority
    });
    $scope.newPriority--;
  }
};

$scope.edit = function(item) {
  $scope.editedItem = item;
  $scope.modal.show();
};

$scope.save = function() {
  $scope.items.$save($scope.editedItem);
  $scope.modal.hide();
  $ionicListDelegate.closeOptionButtons();
};

$scope.close = function() {
  $scope.modal.hide();
  $ionicListDelegate.closeOptionButtons();
};

$scope.delete = function(item) {
  $scope.items.$remove(item);
  $ionicListDelegate.closeOptionButtons();
};
```

Deleting a record is very simple; you just have to call `$scope.items.$remove()`. You can pass an index of the record or the record itself, which is an object reference. You can add a record by calling `$scope.items.$add()` and passing the record content. AngularFire will take care of the entire REST API operation. The `edit()` function here is actually used to just show the modal and assign the item object to `$scope.editedItem`.

The reason behind this assignment is that the modal needs to know which record it is dealing with. So, it's best to make a separate reference and have it available for the modal. Once the user edits the content of this record, `$scope.items.$save()` will take care of the save operation.

6. Go back to the command line to run the app via `ionic serve`.

7. You should be able to see the following in the browser:

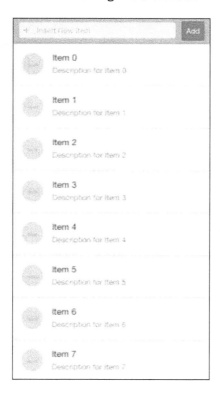

8. Open the browser console to take a look at the array object's output. This is just done so that you understand what is returned to the browser.

9. Navigate to the **Elements** tab of the console. If you scroll down, note that the `<ion-item>` content is actually being updated dynamically. This is the result of using `collection-repeat`, as it only keeps one page of records in the DOM. When you scroll down, `collection-repeat` will update the `<ion-item>` tag instead. This allows infinite scrolling without you realizing that you are going through the content page by page.

```
Q    Elements  Network  Sources  Timeline  Profiles  Resources  Audits  Console
  ▼ <div class="scroll" style="-webkit-transform: translate3d(0px, 0px, 0px) scale(1);">
    ▼ <div class="collection-repeat-container" style="-webkit-transform: translate3d(0px, 0px, 0px);">
        <ion-item collection-repeat="item in items" class="item ng-binding" style="-webkit-transform: translate3d(0px, 54px, 0px); height:
        55px; width: 1280px;">
            1
        </ion-item>
        <ion-item collection-repeat="item in items" class="item ng-binding" style="-webkit-transform: translate3d(-9999px, -9999px, 0px);
        height: 55px; width: 1280px;">
            13
        </ion-item>
        <ion-item collection-repeat="item in items" class="item ng-binding" style="-webkit-transform: translate3d(0px, 162px, 0px);
        height: 55px; width: 1280px;">
            3
        </ion-item>
        <ion-item collection-repeat="item in items" class="item ng-binding" style="-webkit-transform: translate3d(-9999px, -9999px, 0px);
```

How it works...

The app created in the preceding recipe can be very complicated if you build your own backend and frontend code to achieve the same scrolling performance. The key here is to assign `$firebaseArray()` to some object within `$scope` so that you can perform data operations while allowing the function to bind data at the view level. There is no need to create another `ItemViewModel` instance, especially for situations such as when you need to just handle the synchronization between frontend data and the view model.

It's best to use `collection-repeat` whenever possible in your Ionic app. The data in `collection-repeat` must be an array, which is similar to how `ng-repeat` works. You cannot use one-time binding (`::model`), because `collection-repeat` needs to update the model for each item in the list. You don't need to worry about the number of items in the list as well as the height of the item on the screen. Also, it's a good practice to cache images if `<img>` is used for `collection-repeat`.

There's more...

For more information about `collection-repeat`, visit `http://ionicframework.com/docs/api/directive/collectionRepeat/`.

Saving form data to Firebase

This recipe will cover another example of using Firebase as a persistent storage layer for your app. A very common use case that you will see in every app is the ability to have users fill out a form and save data to the server. Sometimes, there is more than one form in the entire process. A good example is a multistep shopping cart checkout app.

You will create an app that will:

- Have three screens with a form per screen
- Allow a user to either swipe or click on the **Back** and **Next** buttons to navigate horizontally to each screen
- Let a user submit the form and save it to Firebase

Getting ready

You can close the previous app from your editor because this example will start with a brand new app.

How to do it...

Here are the steps:

1. Let's start with a blank Ionic app (such as `firebase-ionic-form`) and include `firebase-v2.2.4.js` and `angularfire-v1.1.1.min.js` in the `index.html` header, as follows:

   ```
   $ ionic start firebase-ionic-form blank
   ```

2. Structure the `index.html` file in such a way that it has a header and a body area with a slide box. But first, you need to assign a controller and a full-screen class so that the form can take the entire space of the device screen:

   ```
   <body ng-app="starter" ng-controller="FormCtrl"
   class="full-screen">
   Open /www/css/style.css to add some custom styles
   .full-screen {
     position: fixed;
   }

   body > div.has-header.full-screen {
     height: 100%;
   }

   .slider {
     height: 100%;
   }
   ```

   By default, Ionic's slider will only expand as far as the inner content goes. So, if your content only takes half of the space, Ionic's slider won't expand all the way to the bottom. This means that users cannot swipe if they touch the second half of the screen, because Ionic's slider cannot detect a touch event outside its own covered area.

3. Add the header within the `<body>` tag, as follows:

```html
<div class="bar bar-header">
  <button class="button" ng-if="data.currentSlide > 0"
  ng-click="data.currentSlide = data.currentSlide - 1">
    <i class="icon ion-chevron-left"></i>
    Back
  </button>
  <h1 class="title">Step {{ data.currentSlide + 1 }}</h1>
  <button class="button button-positive"
  ng-if="data.currentSlide < 2" ng-click="data.currentSlide
  = data.currentSlide + 1">
    Next
    <i class="icon ion-chevron-right"></i>
  </button>
  <button class="button button-positive"
  ng-if="data.currentSlide == 2" ng-disabled="data.
  completed" ng-click="submit()">
    Purchase
  </button>
</div>
```

There is a lot going on in this header. But for the most part, the user will see a **Back** and **Next** button. The **Purchase** button only appears when you are on the last slide (which is slide 2) of the slider. The slide box will bind to this `data.currentSlide` variable so that you can get the current value or assign a value to it in order to programmatically change the slide.

4. Insert the following `ion-slide-box` code:

```html
<div class="has-header full-screen">
  <ion-slide-box active-slide="data.currentSlide">
    <ion-slide>
      <div class="list">
        <label class="item item-input">
          <span class="input-label">First</span>
          <input type="text" ng-model="formData.first">
        </label>
        <label class="item item-input">
          <span class="input-label">Last</span>
          <input type="text" ng-model="formData.last">
        </label>
        <label class="item item-input">
          <span class="input-label">Email</span>
          <input type="email" ng-model="formData.email">
        </label>
      </div>
    </ion-slide>
```

```
<ion-slide>
  <div class="list">
    <label class="item item-input">
      <input type="text" pattern="\d*"
      placeholder="Card Number" ng-model="formData.cc">
    </label>
    <label class="item item-input">
      <input type="text" pattern="\d*" placeholder
      ="CVC" maxlength="4" ng-model="formData.cvc">
    </label>
    <label class="item item-input">
      <input type="text" pattern="\d*" placeholder
      ="Expiration" maxlength="4"
      ng-model="formData.exp">
    </label>
  </div>
</ion-slide>
<ion-slide>
  <ul class="list">
    <li class="item item-input item-select">
      <div class="input-label">
        LCD TV
      </div>
      <select ng-model="formData.model">
        <option value="60-in" selected>60
        Inches</option>
        <option value="65-in">65 Inches</option>
        <option value="70-in">70 Inches</option>
      </select>
    </li>
    <li class="item item-toggle">
      Extended Warranty
      <label class="toggle toggle-assertive">
        <input type="checkbox"
        ng-model="formData.warranty">
        <div class="track">
          <div class="handle"></div>
        </div>
      </label>
    </li>
  </ul>
  <h4 class="balanced" ng-if="data.completed">Your
  purchase has been completed!</h4>
</ion-slide>
  </ion-slide-box>
</div>
```

You must declare `active-slide="data.currentSlide"` in order for the slide box directive to know the variable on which to perform two-way binding. The structure of a slide box is similar to `<select>` and `<option>` in HTML. You basically start the group with `<ion-slide-box>`, and for each box, you just need to put the HTML content inside `<ion-slide>`.

> The rest of the code comprises just regular form elements such as select, text, and number inputs. Bind each input with a model such as `formData.first` (that is, first name) or `formData.email` (that is, email).

5. Open `app.js` to edit it. You may want to delete the entire content and insert the following in it:

```
var app = angular.module('starter', ['ionic', 'firebase']);

app.run(function($ionicPlatform, $firebaseArray,
$timeout) {
  $ionicPlatform.ready(function() {
    // Hide the accessory bar by default (remove this
    to show the accessory bar above the keyboard
    // for form inputs)
    if(window.cordova && window.cordova.plugins.Keyboard) {
      cordova.plugins.Keyboard.
      hideKeyboardAccessoryBar(true);
    }
    if(window.StatusBar) {
      StatusBar.styleDefault();
    }
  });
});

app.controller('FormCtrl', function($scope,
$firebaseArray) {
  var ref = new Firebase('https://ionicebook.firebaseio
  .com/transactions/');
  $scope.transactions = $firebaseArray(ref);
  $scope.formData = {};
  $scope.data = {
    completed: false,
    currentSlide: 0
```

```
  };

  // If user changes slide, make notification disappear
  $scope.$watch('data.currentSlide',
  function(newVal, oldVal) {
    if ((newVal < 2) && (oldVal == 2))
      $scope.data.completed = false;
  })

  $scope.submit = function() {
    // Check if the form is "dirty" or not as user
    must fill out something
    if (angular.equals({}, $scope.formData)) {
      alert("Your form is empty");
    } else {
      // Add the entire $scope.formData object to
      Firebase and reset it
      $scope.transactions.$add($scope.formData).
      then(function(res) {
        $scope.formData = {};
        $scope.data.completed = true;
        // Mark "completed" to show the notification
        in view
      });
    }
  };
});
```

Your `FormCtrl` controller is very simple in this case. In a real-world application, there are more steps to validate the form data. For example, the customer name must be alphabetical in nature and a credit card's expiration date must be valid. However, this section will not delve into validation. The focus here is to explain how to just send *data* to Firebase by calling the `$scope.transactions.$add()` function.

6. Run the app and fill out some fake data in the form, as follows:

7. Click on **Purchase**, and you will see the **Your purchase has been completed!** confirmation text. This means that the app has successfully sent the data to Firebase and all the form models are reset:

8. To confirm that the data existed in Firebase, go to your Firebase app and look at the `transactions` node. You will see a JSON, like the following screenshot:

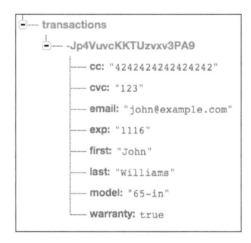

This means that all the form data has been saved successfully to your Firebase app.

How it works...

The simple example in the preceding section helps demonstrate a few key concepts. These concepts are as follows:

▸ You can have multiple forms using any method such as a slide box or another route in a Single-Page Application structure. You can save data to Firebase in the last step using one simple call to `$add()`.

▸ By default, Ionic's slide box does not cover the entire screen. You may want to modify some styles to change this behavior.

▸ Form data is just a JSON model. You can bind each value to an input box.

- The `active-slide` option of `<ion-slide-box>` is the two-way data binding. So, you can get the current slide or change it to make the slide box jump to a particular slide.

- There are many ways that can be used to detect the *state* of your form: `empty`, `valid`, `invalid`, `submitted`, and so on. The preceding example does not go deep into validation but just provides a few easy paths to check the state using the `data.currentSlide` or `data.completed` variables.

In addition to this, note the use of the `$scope.$watch('data.currentSlide', function(newVal, oldVal)` in the controller. Since the app provides users with two ways to navigate each slide (either click on the **Back** and **Next** button, or swipe), you need to actually bind data to the live value of the slide number. So, if the user navigates away from the last slide (which is slide 2), you basically tell the view to hide the notification text. By default, the text does not appear until after the `submit()` function is called.

10

Finalizing Your Apps for Different Platforms

In this chapter, we will cover the following tasks related to building and publishing apps:

- ▸ Building and publishing an app for iOS
- ▸ Building and publishing an app for Android
- ▸ Using PhoneGap Build for cross-platform applications

Introduction

In the past, it used to be very cumbersome to build and successfully publish an app. However, there is much documentation and many unofficial instructions on the Internet today that can pretty much address any problem that you may run into. In addition, Ionic also comes with its own CLI to assist in this process. This chapter will guide you through the app building and publishing steps at a high level. You will learn how to:

- ▸ Build an iOS and Android app via the Ionic CLI
- ▸ Publish an iOS app using Xcode via iTunes Connect
- ▸ Build a Windows Phone app using PhoneGap Build

The purpose of this chapter is to provide ideas on what to look for and some *gotchas*. Apple, Google, and Microsoft are constantly updating their platforms and processes. So, the steps may not look exactly the same over time.

Building and publishing an app for iOS

Publishing on the App Store can be a frustrating process if you are not well prepared upfront. In this recipe, we will go through the steps that are required to properly configure everything in the Apple Developer Center, iTunes Connect, and a local Xcode project.

Getting ready

You must register for the Apple Developer Program in order to access `https://developer.apple.com` and `https://itunesconnect.apple.com` because these websites will require an approved account.

In addition to this, the instructions in the subsequent recipes use the latest version of the following components:

- Mac OS X Yosemite 10.10.4
- Xcode 6.4
- Ionic CLI 1.6.4
- Cordova 5.1.1

How to do it...

Here are the instructions to build and publish an app for iOS:

1. Make sure that you are in the `app` folder and build for the iOS platform:

   `$ ionic build ios`

2. Go to the `ios` folder `/platforms` and open the `.xcodeproj` file in Xcode:

3. Go through the **General** tab to make sure that you have the correct information for everything, especially the information related to Bundle Identifier and version. Change and save this as needed:

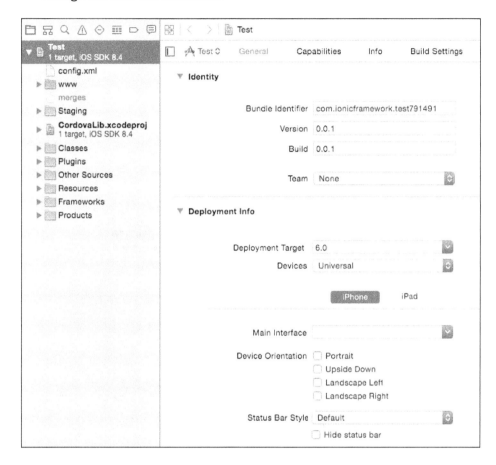

4. Visit the Apple Developer website and click on **Certificates, Identifiers & Profiles**:

Certificates, Identifiers & Profiles

Manage your certificates, identifiers, devices, and profiles for your apps.

5. For an iOS app, you just have to go through the steps on the website and fill out the necessary information:

The important part that you need to do correctly here is, going to **Identifiers** | **App IDs** because it must match your Bundle Identifier in Xcode.

6. Visit iTunes Connect and select the **My Apps** button:

7. Select the Plus (+) icon and click on **New iOS App**:

8. Fill out the form and make sure that you select the right Bundle Identifier for your app:

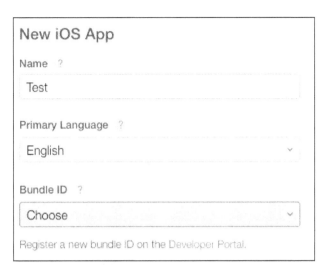

There are several additional steps that require you to provide information about the app such as screenshot, icon, address, and so on. If you just want to test the app, you can just provide some placeholder information initially and come back to edit it later.

That's it when it comes to preparing your Developer and iTunes Connect account.

9. Now, open Xcode and select **iOS Device** as the archive target. Otherwise, the Archive feature will not be turned on. You will need to archive your app before you can submit it to the App Store.

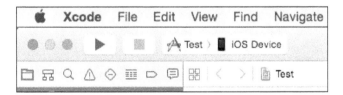

10. Navigate to **Product | Archive** in the menu at the top:

11. After the archive process is completed, select **Submit to App Store** to finish the publishing process.

12. At first, the app may take an hour to appear in iTunes Connect. However, subsequent submissions will happen faster. You should look for the build in the **iOS App 1.0 Prepare for Submission** menu in iTunes Connect. Then select the build version (which is 0.0.1 in this case) and click on the **Done** button.:

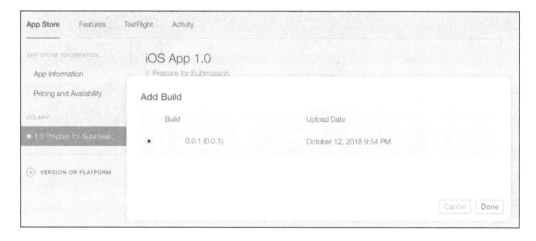

iTunes Connect has a very nice integration with TestFlight to test your app. You can switch this feature on and off. Note that for each publication, you have to change the version number in Xcode so that it won't conflict with the existing version in iTunes Connect.

13. To publish the app, select **Submit for Beta App Review**. You may want to go through other tabs such as Pricing and In-App Purchases to configure your own requirements.

How it works...

This recipe obviously does not cover every bit of detail in the publishing process. In general, you just need to make sure that your app is locally tested thoroughly in a physical device (either via USB or TestFlight) before submitting it to the App Store.

If for some reason the Archive feature doesn't build, you can manually go to the local Xcode folder to delete the specific temporarily archived app to clear the cache, as follows:

`~/Library/Developer/Xcode/Archives`

See also

TestFlight is a separate subject in itself. The benefit of TestFlight is that you don't need your app to be approved by Apple in order to install the app on a physical device for internal testing and development. You can find out more about TestFlight at `https://developer.apple.com/library/prerelease/ios/documentation/LanguagesUtilities/Conceptual/iTunesConnect_Guide/Chapters/BetaTestingTheApp.html`.

Building and publishing an app for Android

Building and publishing an Android app is a little more straightforward than iOS because you just interface with the command line to build an `.apk` file and upload it to Google Play Developer Console. The Ionic Framework documentation also has a great instruction page for this, which can be viewed by visiting `http://ionicframework.com/docs/guide/publishing.html`.

Getting ready

The requirement is to have your Google Developer account ready and log in to `https://play.google.com/apps/publish`. Your local environment should also have the right SDK as well as the keytool, jarsigner, and zipalign command line for that specific version.

How to do it...

Here are the instructions to build and publish an app for Android:

1. Go to your `app` folder and build the release for Android:

   ```
   $ ionic build --release android
   ```

2. You will see `android-release-unsigned.apk` in the `apk` folder under `/platforms/android/build/outputs`. Go to this folder in the Terminal:

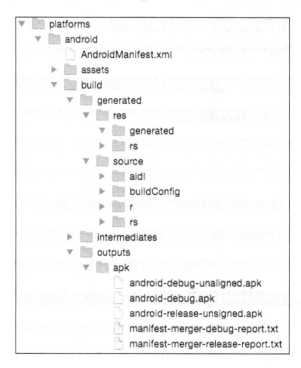

3. If you're creating this app for the first time, you must have a keystore file. This file is used to identify your app for publishing. If you lose it, you cannot update your app later on. To create a keystore, type the following command line and make sure that it's the same keytool version of the SDK:

```
$ keytool -genkey -v -keystore my-release-key.keystore -alias
alias_name -keyalg RSA -keysize 2048 -validity 10000
```

4. Once you fill out the information in the command line, make a copy of this file and keep it somewhere safe because you will need it later.

5. The next step is to use this file to *sign* your app so that it will create a new `.apk` file that Google Play allows users to install:

```
$ jarsigner -verbose -sigalg SHA1withRSA -digestalg SHA1 -keystore
my-release-key.keystore HelloWorld-release-unsigned.apk alias_name
```

6. To prepare for the final `.apk` file before upload, you must package it using `zipalign`, as follows:

```
$ zipalign -v 4 HelloWorld-release-unsigned.apk HelloWorld.apk
```

 You must use the correct version of zipalign tool based on the Android SDK version. For Mac users, if you picked SDK v22, the zipalign path will be very likely at /Users/[YOUR USERNAME]/Library/ Android/sdk/build-tools/22.0.1/.

7. Log in to the Google Developer Console and select **Add new application**:

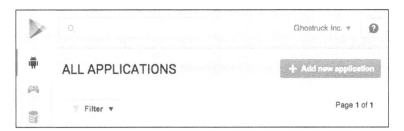

8. Fill out as much information for your app as possible using the menu to the left:

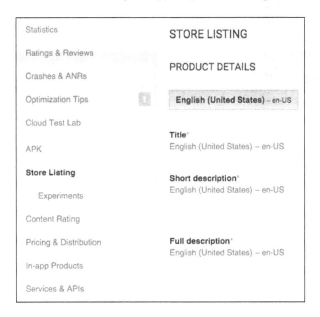

9. Now, you are ready to upload the `.apk` file. First perform a Beta test:

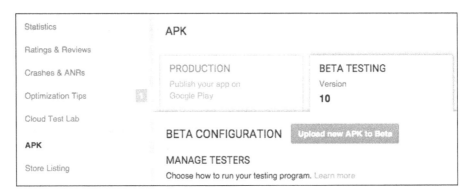

10. Once you are done with Beta testing, you can follow the Developer Console instructions to push the app to **Production**.

How it works...

This recipe does not cover other Android marketplaces such as Amazon Appstore because each of them has different processes. However, the common idea is that you need to completely build the unsigned version of `.apk`, sign it using an existing or new keystore file, and finally zipalign to prepare for upload.

Using PhoneGap Build for cross-platform applications

Adobe PhoneGap Build is a very useful product that provides *build-as-a-service* in the cloud. If you are having trouble building an app locally in your computer, you can upload the entire Ionic project to PhoneGap Build, and it will build the app for Apple, Android, and Windows Phone automatically.

Getting ready

Go to `https://build.phonegap.com` and register for a free account. You will be able to build one private app for free. For additional private apps, there is a monthly fee associated with the account.

How to do it...

Here are the instructions to use PhoneGap Build for cross-platform applications:

1. Zip the entire `/www` folder and replace `cordova.js` with `phonegap.js` in `index.html`, as described in `http://docs.build.phonegap.com/en_US/introduction_getting_started.md.html#Getting%20Started%20with%20Build`.

2. You may have to edit `config.xml` to ensure that all the plugins are included. Detailed changes are available in PhoneGap documentation, which can be viewed by visiting `http://docs.build.phonegap.com/en_US/configuring_plugins.md.html#Plugins`.

3. Select `Upload a .zip file` under the **private** tab:

4. Upload the ZIP file of the www folder.

5. Make sure that you upload an appropriate key for each platform. For a Windows Phone, upload the publisher ID file.

6. After this, you just build the app and download the completed build file for each platform.

How it works...

In a nutshell, PhoneGap Build is a convenient way of building apps when you are only familiar with one platform during the development process but you want your app to be built quickly for other platforms. Under the hood, PhoneGap Build has its own environment to automate the process for each user. However, the user still has to own the responsibility of providing a key file to sign the app. PhoneGap Build just helps you attach the key to your app.

See also

A common issue that people face when using PhoneGap Build is a failure to build. You may want to refer to their documentation to troubleshoot. This documentation is available at `http://docs.build.phonegap.com/en_US/support_failed-builds.md.html#Failed%20Builds`.

Index

Symbol

$scope.$digest() function 92

A

addUser() function 117
AngularFire API
  reference 210
AngularJS
  controller 5
  directive 5
  filter 6
  service 6
app
  animating, requestAnimationFrame using with
      event binding 160-167
  building, for Android 233-236
  building, for iOS 228-232
  publishing, for Android 233-236
  publishing, for iOS 228-232
array data
  saving, to Firebase 210-212

B

blank template
  Ionic, setting up with 5

C

communication, between various components
  controller to directive 126
  directive to factory 126
  enabling, events used 126-134

factory to factory 126
state to view and/or controller 126
view to controller 126
view to view 126
contact
  adding 74-80
  picking 73-81
Cordova
  URL 57
Cordova Google Maps plugin
  features 93
  reference 81
Cordova Video Player plugin
  URL 68
CSS3 filters
  URL 64
custom filter
  creating 155-159

D

development environment
  setting up 2-4
device camera
  used, for capturing photo 58-63
drag events
  detecting, with gesture coordinate 120-125

E

email
  composing with attachment, from app 68-72
examples
  copying, from Ionic Codepen Demos 11, 12

N

ngCordova
URL 57
Node.js
URL 2

O

out-of-the-box filters
reference 155

P

Package Control
about 3
URL 3
PhoneGap Build
about 236
URL 236
using, for cross-platform
applications 236-238
working 237
photo
capturing, device camera used 58-63
Plugin Manager 3
progress bars 150
promise 116

S

scroll progress bar directive
creating 150-152
working 153, 154
setCenterLocation() function 92
sidemenu template
app, creating with 5

social networking app
creating, with SQLite 103-118
standard templates
about 4
blank 4
sidemenu 4
tabs 4
Sublime Text
about 3
URL 3

T

tab interface
creating, with nested views 34-41
themes
customizing, for specific platforms 136-138
to-do app
creating with ngStorage,
for Local Storage 96-103
Twitter app
configuring, with Firebase
authentication 176-179

U

updateGroupByUserId() function 117

V

Velocity.js
URL 167
video
capturing 64-67
playback, allowing 64-67
Videogular
URL 68

Thank you for buying
Ionic Cookbook

About Packt Publishing

Packt, pronounced 'packed', published its first book, *Mastering phpMyAdmin for Effective MySQL Management*, in April 2004, and subsequently continued to specialize in publishing highly focused books on specific technologies and solutions.

Our books and publications share the experiences of your fellow IT professionals in adapting and customizing today's systems, applications, and frameworks. Our solution-based books give you the knowledge and power to customize the software and technologies you're using to get the job done. Packt books are more specific and less general than the IT books you have seen in the past. Our unique business model allows us to bring you more focused information, giving you more of what you need to know, and less of what you don't.

Packt is a modern yet unique publishing company that focuses on producing quality, cutting-edge books for communities of developers, administrators, and newbies alike. For more information, please visit our website at www.packtpub.com.

About Packt Open Source

In 2010, Packt launched two new brands, Packt Open Source and Packt Enterprise, in order to continue its focus on specialization. This book is part of the Packt open source brand, home to books published on software built around open source licenses, and offering information to anybody from advanced developers to budding web designers. The Open Source brand also runs Packt's open source Royalty Scheme, by which Packt gives a royalty to each open source project about whose software a book is sold.

Writing for Packt

We welcome all inquiries from people who are interested in authoring. Book proposals should be sent to author@packtpub.com. If your book idea is still at an early stage and you would like to discuss it first before writing a formal book proposal, then please contact us; one of our commissioning editors will get in touch with you.

We're not just looking for published authors; if you have strong technical skills but no writing experience, our experienced editors can help you develop a writing career, or simply get some additional reward for your expertise.

Mastering Kendo UI [Video]

ISBN: 978-1-78398-946-1   Duration: 01:30 hours

Tap into the full power of the Kendo UI framework and its widgets with this clear and concise guide

1. Make the most of MVVM, Kendo UI, and Bootstrap to build a fully functional blogging application.

2. Configure the most popular Kendo UI widgets to improve the functionality of your app.

3. Put Telerik's backend services to work and store your data safely for when you need it.

Kendo UI Cookbook

ISBN: 978-1-78398-000-0   Paperback: 250 pages

Over 50 recipes to help you rapidly build rich and dynamic user interfaces for web and mobile platforms

1. Create rich interfaces for the Web using the Kendo UI application framework and various sets of widgets that come packaged in the library.

2. Build web applications for the mobile platform by providing a native look and feel on iOS, Android, Blackberry, and Windows Phone, without having to worry about maintaining separate codebases for each platform.

3. Leverage HTML5-based DataViz widgets in the Kendo UI library to build charts and dashboards.

Please check **www.PacktPub.com** for information on our titles

Learning Kendo UI Web Development

ISBN: 978-1-84969-434-6   Paperback: 288 pages

An easy-to-follow practical tutorial to add exciting features to your web pages without being a JavaScript expert

1. Learn from clear and specific examples on how to utilize the full range of the Kendo UI tool set for the web.

2. Add powerful tools to your website supported by a familiar and trusted name in innovative technology.

3. Learn how to add amazing features with clear examples and make your website more interactive without being a JavaScript expert.

Sencha Touch Cookbook,
Second Edition

ISBN: 978-1-78216-918-5   Paperback: 418 pages

Over 100 hands-on recipes to help you understand the complete Sencha Touch framework and solve your day-to-day problems

1. Learn every aspect of creating, building, packaging, and running a Sencha Touch application.

2. Integrate your applications with different data sources and present them differently using list, data view, charts, and so on.

3. Package your application with or without Cordova/PhoneGap and run them on a desktop, emulator, and a real mobile device.

Please check **www.PacktPub.com** for information on our titles